One Part Plant

One Part Plant

A SIMPLE GUIDE TO EATING REAL, ONE MEAL AT A TIME

Jessica Murnane

HARPER WAVE

An Imprint of HarperCollins*Publishers*

HarperCollins
PUBLISHERS

FIRST EDITION

Photographs by Nicole Franzen

Food and Prop Styling by Vivian Lui and Joni Noe

Butternut Squash Soup recipe slightly adapted from *My Kitchen Year: 136 Recipes That Saved My Life* by Ruth Reichl, copyright © 2015 by Ruth Reichl. Used by permission of Random House, an imprint and division of Penguin Random House LLC. All rights reserved.

Designed by Leah Carlson-Stanisic

Patterns by TrishaMcmillan/Shutterstock, Inc., Kvanta/Shutterstock, Inc., Daria Rosen/Shutterstock, Inc., stuckmotion/Shutterstock, Inc., Angry_red_cat/Shutterstock, Inc.

Library of Congress Cataloging-in-Publication Data has been applied for.

ISBN 978-0-06-244061-7

17 18 19 20 21   QGT   10 9 8 7 6 5 4 3 2 1

To Amanda

CONTENTS

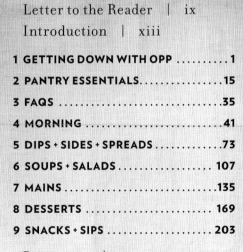

Letter to the Reader

from Lena Dunham

Dear Reader,

Welcome to a really good book. Seriously, you don't know what's about to hit you—this book is joyful, playful, delicious, and guess what? It will also change your life.

Let me start by saying I'm no saint in the food department. When doctors act impressed that I don't smoke or drink, I always say, "But you haven't asked about cheese yet." Like so many people, so many women, my life has been a struggle between what tastes right to me and what IS right FOR me. Even during a decade-long dalliance with veganism, my regimen consisted of French fries, Sprite, and veggie dogs on massive fluffy buns. My boyfriend describes my dietary preferences as "three-year-old with a credit card."

When endometriosis entered my life full throttle, I knew I had to make some adjustments as I dealt with a chronic disease, but it was hard to admit those changes might be dietary. When you're already exhausted, stressed, and pissed at Lady God, you don't also want your Bolognese and biscuits taken away from you. I was a ravenous beast clinging to quesadillas for dear life.

But after I decided to go public with my struggle, a little angel reached out her hand in the form of one Ms. Jessica Murnane. Without preaching, without judgment, she sent me a list of some of the food changes that had worked for her in her own journey with the illness. I'm pretty public with my challenges, so I get a lot of random emails from people making suggestions (their acupuncturist, their pet psychic, the Wiccan crystal shop that got them pregnant), but something about Jessica's tone drew me to her. She wasn't making a big list of don'ts, but rather introducing a whole new world of mysterious ingredients and exciting kitchen adventures. A plant-based Hogwarts, if you will. She also readily admitted that she hadn't started out as a domestic goddess and that change is a bitch.

Armed with a Jessica-approved shopping list, I started making some changes of my own. Instead of Greek yogurt with half a squeeze bottle of honey, I was enjoying coconut yogurt with a mess of berries and seeds. Instead of toast with peanut butter, there was sprouted Ezekiel bread with black sesame and preserves. I sent her photos of every silly experiment, and she cheered me on like a kindergarten art teacher. I loved that her philosophy made room for slipups, and furthermore, she didn't even label them as such. She didn't label AT all.

Her natural approach also encouraged me to start asking questions about what was going on my face and body. As someone who spends more time in a makeup chair than I ever dreamed possible, it had never occurred to me that the pounds of foundations, mascara, and Aqua Net that are applied to me on the regular might be just as shitty for my system as gas station beef jerky. But Jessica is that friend who always has the better way (while totally acknowledging how shitty the new way can feel). She said, in no uncertain terms, that I was allowed to miss birthday cake ice cream and Lady Speed Stick. I was even allowed to fuck with them sometimes. But small changes are still changes, and you will feel them in ways that surprise and excite you.

So I invite you to follow Jessica into the vast green wilderness—the secret is it's not so scary, just healthy. And fun. All our journeys with our bodies will have a million twists and turns, but knowledge arms us to handle them with aplomb. And there's a lot of knowledge in here, from a lady who learned it the hard way while still making it look easy. Thank you, Jess.

Viva la plant,
Lena

Introduction

When I was on my way home from the airport recently, my cabdriver asked me what I did for a living. I told him that I used to be a designer, but then a few years ago, I completely shifted my career and now have a podcast and would be publishing a cookbook soon. He perked up when I mentioned the cookbook and told me he loved to cook and was a bit of a chef himself. He asked me what kind of cookbook I was writing and about the types of food I loved to cook. I told him it was going to be a plant-based cookbook. "Oh," he said as if I'd crushed all his dreams (and my dreams of him preordering this thing). I went into full hype-woman mode and told him that plant-based eating can be really delicious. I shared some of my favorite recipes, described the gorgeous photos in these pages, and even name-dropped some of the big chefs who were contributing to the book. But I could tell he was starting to tune me out. Before he stopped paying attention completely, he did ask one question:

"Why would you eat a plant-based diet, anyway?"

I told him I hadn't actually wanted to change my diet, and in fact, I'd fought against it pretty hard at first. But five years ago, I was headed for a hysterectomy at the age of thirty-three, because of my Stage 4 endometriosis. I couldn't get out of bed most mornings because my pain had become so severe. I did everything I could to get better. I underwent multiple surgeries; I tried conventional painkillers and less-conventional ones (I was a stoner for a month, but it really wasn't my thing), fancy yoga and not-so-fancy yoga, and even therapy to help with the depression that comes with chronic pain. Nothing worked.

I hit my lowest point, I told him, when my doctors said they were out of solutions to help me manage my pain and advised me to undergo a hysterectomy. As scary as it was, I agreed to move forward with the surgery because I thought it would end my pain. But soon after that, I received an email from a friend that changed my life. She sent me a link to a website that explained how eating a plant-based diet could help alleviate some of the pain and symptoms of endometriosis. I had never even seen the phrase "plant-based" before, and I was pretty skeptical about the whole thing. I mean, if the right nutrition could help me, why hadn't my doctors told me this? And then I read what I had to eat. No candy? No cheese? No fun? I had zero faith that the diet would work, and whatever-is-less-than-zero faith that I could actually stick to whatever this plant-based thing was. But I'm also a people pleaser, and I didn't really actually want to have the surgery. So I told my friend I would give it a try.

And it worked.

Within weeks, my pain began to fade. After a month, my eyes seemed to open a little wider, and I had more energy. Within three months, I was a completely different person. After six months, my husband said I had "my sparkle back." I conquered the insomnia that had plagued me for a dozen years. I finally got a handle on my depression. I felt the best I'd ever felt—and I told my doctors I didn't need that hysterectomy after all.

I'd gotten my cabbie's interest. He turned around, looked me right in the eye, and said, "Next time, you should really lead with that."

Damn.

He was right. This book isn't just about plant-based recipes, really pretty photos, and inspiring chefs. This is also a story of how real food transformed my life from the inside out. That's the reason I'm writing this book. So, yeah. I guess I'm leading with that.

Five years ago, if you'd told me what my life would look like now, I wouldn't have believed you.

I'm writing a cookbook? Wait. I cook? What kind of cookbook? Plant-based food? What in thhheee—VEGETABLES? Noooooo. You're joking? I like them? Because of them, I'm not in pain anymore? I didn't get a hysterectomy? I'm not sad? I love my life? Can you get me a tissue? Yes, I'm crying! No, they're happy tears!

Even now, it doesn't feel real. But, man, I'm so glad it is. Changing my diet truly changed my life, and I want everyone—sick, healthy, and in between—to have the opportunity to benefit from real food in the same way that I did. With this book, I want to provide you with the tools and support to get started on that journey.

Now, we might not know each other very well yet, but the fact that you picked up this book tells me a lot about you. You want to shake things up and do something a little different for yourself. Which makes me really excited, and I want to hug you so hard. Because I know from making that same choice that changing your eating habits even just a *little* bit can make a *huge* difference in your quality of life. I also know that it can be hard to make these changes on your own, so that's why I'm here. Because I believe in the healing power of real food, and I believe in you.

Let's get started already.

Love, Jessica

One Part Plant

1 | Getting Down with OPP

What does One Part Plant (OPP) mean? OPP is an eating philosophy; it means at least *one* meal a day is made up of real, whole, plant-based foods. One. OPP is not some crazy diet with a list of forbidden foods you can never eat again, and it doesn't require you to join a culty food tribe with a million rules. OPP is about making plants the star of the show for one meal a day. Breakfast, lunch, or dinner—you pick. Once a day you'll create, pick up, or order in (no shame in that) a plant-based meal.

But let's back up for a second. If you're not familiar with the terms *whole foods* or *plant-based,* the concept is pretty simple. Whole foods are foods that are minimally processed or not processed at all—veggies, fruits, nuts, seeds, grains, and legumes. *Plant-based* means that these foods come from the ground and the trees and are not derived from animals (although many plant-based eaters consume honey, myself included).

I try really hard to avoid talking too much about the foods you CAN'T eat on a plant-based diet. For starters, I'm not here to tell you what you can and can't eat—as far as I'm concerned, it's your choice to eat whatever you want. But more importantly, rattling off a list of "bad foods" isn't a great way to get excited about a new way of eating; I know I'd prefer to focus on all of the things I *can* eat rather than the foods that are off limits. That said, it wouldn't make a lot of sense if I didn't explain why certain foods—for example, ones that start with *ch* and end with *eese*—are not considered to be part of a plant-based diet and are not included in OPP.

That reason is inflammation.

Doctors, nutritionists, and dieticians have been debating for years what *the best* diet is for overall health. And the results of that debate are, well, confusing. There's so much information out there that it's hard to find a single theory that everyone can agree on. But one idea remains pretty consistent in every camp: inflammatory foods are not our friends. Chronic inflammation has been linked to cancer, heart disease, diabetes, arthritis, depression, and Alzheimer's. We also know that women with endometriosis can experience more severe symptoms when they consume inflammatory foods. And even if you are fortunate enough to never experience one of these major illnesses, there's still a pretty good chance that inflammation will get in the way of you feeling your absolute best in some other way—like persistent skin problems or digestive issues.

So what are inflammatory foods? The main culprits include processed and packaged foods, dairy products, red meat, sugar, fried foods, soda, refined carbohydrates (pastries, white bread), and alcohol. You may have noticed some of your favorite foods in this list, and that's OK. Right now, I'm simply identifying and sharing them with you. By becoming more aware of these foods, you can pay attention to how they're making you feel when you eat them.

One other note about inflammatory foods: some people experience inflammation after eating grains, corn, soy, and nightshade vegetables (eggplant, peppers, tomatoes, and potatoes). Each of us has a unique body, and we all react uniquely to different foods, even those that are widely considered to be "healthy." Again, the important thing is not to swear off all of these foods completely, but to gain an awareness of how your body reacts when you eat them.

Wait a second, you may be thinking. *You forgot about gluten. Isn't that THE biggest cause of inflammation?!*

I know, I know. I was just getting to that.

When it comes to gluten, everyone has an opinion. Some experts say it's the worst thing you could possibly put in your body, and others that say it's perfectly safe. New studies with contradictory findings seem to make headlines every day, and it's hard to keep up with all of the evolving research on gluten, let alone know if it's safe to eat a piece of bread.

Personally, I don't include much gluten in my diet. For my body, it can cause pretty serious inflammation, which isn't great for endometriosis. I eat it on occasion, maybe once a month. But just because I'm (almost) gluten-free doesn't mean that you need to swear off gluten. So in an effort to offer you the best information I can find on this topic, I asked a doctor I trust—Thomas Campbell, MD (author of *The China Study Solution*)—to share his thoughts. Here's a summary of our conversation:

JM: Can someone be sensitive to gluten—i.e., have some adverse reactions to it—and not necessarily be allergic to it?

TC: There are three types of reactions with gluten: allergies, autoimmune (celiac), and non-celiac gluten sensitivity. Some people do have problems with gluten without having allergies or celiac disease. It's important to note that many of these people are likely to be sensitive to other foods as well, notably dairy.

JM: How do you know if you are sensitive to gluten but don't have celiac disease or an allergy?

TC: There are no good, reliable tests to make a definitive diagnosis of non-celiac gluten sensitivity. The best test is to find a program where you can get exposure to gluten without knowing it while tracking your symptoms. In studies, researchers give patients muffins or other baked items. Some contain gluten, and some do not. Then they track their patients' symptoms and see if the gluten exposure actually provokes symptoms. Interestingly, a majority of patients who feel they have non-celiac gluten sensitivity actually show no correlation between symptoms and gluten exposure when they are tested in this way. In the absence of this type of testing, which removes the placebo effect, people can simply try a gluten-free diet and see how they feel. I do suggest people talk to their doctor first to get tested for celiac. You cannot test for celiac in a reliable way if you are already on a gluten-free diet. So see your doctor before making the switch.

JM: Why does gluten get such a bum rap?

TC: Gluten has been the target of several popular diet books that suggest people should eat a low-carbohydrate diet. There is a slight kernel of truth to these books at the start, but they go on to reach conclusions with which I strongly disagree. One of the most overconsumed foods, usually in the form of highly processed items, is refined flour. Cookies, cakes, pastries, white bread, white pasta, pizza—these are all junk foods that contain lots of unhealthy ingredients above and beyond refined flour. If you get rid of them, you'll be healthier. But it's a remarkable stretch to say that nearly all of our health problems are specifically due to gluten, as these popular books tend to do.

So: the choice is yours. Because I know that my tummy is pretty sensitive to gluten, I eat gluten in moderation and usually stick to gluten-free grains, gluten-free flours, and sprouted breads (I've found these don't cause me as much trouble). The recipes you'll see in this book are intended to be made with breads and grains that are gluten-free, sprouted, or fermented. But that doesn't mean that you have to follow every recipe the way I would. If you want to sub in some whole wheat bread in place of gluten-free bread, go for it. Or if you'd rather have some barley or farro in your curry bowl instead of brown rice, I won't judge.

If you do decide to go 100 percent gluten-free, a word of warning: beware of all of the "gluten-free" packaged products out there and read labels very carefully. A lot of brands remove the gluten from a food but then replace it with a whole slew of ingredients that might make you feel even worse (examples of these are processed starches, soy, and various sugars). In general, if you're eliminating gluten from your diet, I recommend eating foods that are naturally gluten-free instead of foods that are altered to be that way.

I don't want all this talk about gluten and inflammatory foods to scare you away. Remember, we're starting with just one plant-based meal a day—it doesn't have to be every meal. After changing my own diet, I know that subscribing to an all-or-nothing approach is a recipe for failure. Labeling the way we eat doesn't help much either, and there's a lot of labeling these days—paleo, raw, fruitarian, ketogenic, and lots more. When we label the way we eat, it can slowly become not just a diet but our personal identity, too. And then when we go off course and eat some grains or a piece of cheese, we feel that we've failed.

I don't ever want you to feel like you've failed. In fact, I want the idea of eating One Part Plant to give you a little breathing room to be less hard on yourself. It's not about being perfect. It's about adding more real food to your diet, one meal at a time. It's about taking one step every single day to feeling your best. Because when plants become the centerpiece of one meal a day, you will notice significant improvements in the way you feel.

I know I'm making this all sound so easy and breezy—and the reality is, changing your eating habits can be a challenge. There was certainly nothing easy or breezy about it for me. It was emotional. I questioned whether it was worth it. I had a lot of low moments when I wondered if just getting the surgery would be easier than changing the food on my plate. So what kept me going? I was feeling the results of my efforts every day. The damn plant-based thing was working. Real food works.

By changing my diet, I was able to manage the pain from my endometriosis that had interfered with my happiness, career, and relationships for more than a decade. I slept well. My skin looked great, and so did my hair. I had more energy than ever before. I WAS HAPPY for the first time in years. This change also opened my eyes to other ways I could treat myself better—I did my best to stop with the negative self-talk, I began to remove the not-so-positive relationships from my life, figured out ways to manage my stress better, and I began exercising more. All of this work was starting to pay off, so I had to make a choice: gummy bears or my well-being? It was a tough one, but I chose me.

This book contains everything I've learned (with some help from other folks too) about eating, living, and feeling better. I've made all the mistakes, done all of the experimenting, and put in the legwork so you don't have to. So let's get started—with just one meal a day. Give it a shot, and we'll go from there, OK? And we'll definitely throw in some pie along the way.

What Is Endometriosis, Anyway?

———

I didn't want this to be an "endometriosis book." Not because the topic isn't important to me—it's actually what led me here. It's that I believe a plant-based diet has the potential to help more people than just women with endo and don't want to exclude anyone from the conversation.

But there's no way that I'm not going to take the opportunity to dedicate a part of my book to the disease which, according to the Endometriosis Foundation of America, affects 176 million women worldwide (one out of ten women in the US). Sadly many of these women will never be diagnosed even after multiple visits to the doctor. Over the course of a typical woman's journey, she will be made to feel that it's all in her head, that she's weak, that she's just sensitive, or even worse, mentally unstable. In many cases, she will either be ignored or misdiagnosed and medicated for a disease or condition she doesn't actually have.

Endometriosis isn't just about having a "bad period." It affects a woman's career, relationships, and even her ability to participate in simple, everyday activities. The pain is debilitating, yet women push through it and remain silent. It's heartbreaking and unacceptable that they continue to suffer this way, and education is the only way we can create more awareness and begin to help women who endure this disease every day.

If you're reading this and thinking that it doesn't apply to you, I hear you. But please keep reading. My guess is that you know at least one woman in your life. If there's even a small chance that this information could help her or another woman she knows, it's worth the read.

If you're reading this and think you might have endometriosis, find a doctor who specializes in endo or one you feel will take the time to listen to your symptoms and needs and can refer you to a specialist. If you know you have endo and aren't seeing any progress with your symptoms, find a new doctor. Look for one who is well versed in the latest in endo research and surgeries. You'd be surprised how many doctors aren't. Also look for someone who is open to talking about alternative therapies like diet, nutrition, and holistic wellness practices. These are not cures, but anything that could make you feel the slightest bit better is worth a shot.

What Is Endometriosis?

Endometriosis is a disease that occurs when tissue similar to the tissue lining the uterus grows on other parts of the body. It usually grows around the ovaries, bowel, or the tissue lining the pelvis, although it some cases it can spread beyond the pelvic region. During the menstrual cycle, this displaced tissue thickens, breaks down, and bleeds. Because this tissue has no way to exit the body, it becomes trapped. This can lead to cyst formation, adhesions, and severe pain.

What Are the Symptoms?

Symptoms vary from woman to woman, so she might experience one or all of these.

PELVIC PAIN

VERY PAINFUL PERIODS (CRAMPING, LOWER BACK AND ABDOMINAL PAIN)

PAIN DURING OR AFTER SEX

BLOOD CLOTS

PAINFUL BOWEL MOVEMENTS

DIARRHEA AND CONSTIPATION

URINARY FREQUENCY, RETENTION, OR URGENCY

EXCESSIVE BLEEDING

INFERTILITY (THOUGH MANY WOMEN CAN STILL HAVE CHILDREN)

FATIGUE

BLOATING AND GASSINESS

NAUSEA AND VOMITING

OTHER IMMUNE-RELATED ISSUES

How Is It Diagnosed?

According to the documentary *Endo What?*, it takes an average of eight doctors over ten years for a woman to be diagnosed with endometriosis. At some point during this journey, she is commonly misdiagnosed with irritable bowel syndrome (IBS), colon or ovarian cancer, appendicitis, sexually transmitted diseases, or even panic disorder.

Proper diagnosis requires a surgical biopsy, typically involving an outpatient procedure called laparoscopy.

Is There a Cure?

There is no cure, but there are treatments that can help manage symptoms and pain.

What Are the Treatment and Pain Management Plans?

LAPAROSCOPIC SURGERY

DIET AND NUTRITION

ALTERNATIVE THERAPIES (INCLUDING ACUPUNCTURE, EXERCISE, AND MASSAGE)

*HORMONE TREATMENT

*PAINKILLERS

You can find more information on endometriosis and recommendations for further reading in the "Resources" section on page 219.

* I am not endorsing hormone treatment or painkillers, simply stating these are common treatments.

Three Things I Want You to Know Before You Go OPP

1 **Change can feel weird and expensive.** There might be some ingredients in this book that you've never heard of. Up until five years ago, I'd never heard of them either. When I first decided to change my diet, if I saw an ingredient I didn't recognize in a recipe or cooking technique I'd never tried before, I'd roll my eyes and keep on flipping or scrolling until I found one that was familiar. This was also right around the time I started exclusively eating salsa tacos (which are sadly exactly what they sound like—salsa on a taco shell), spaghetti, and frozen gluten-free waffles for almost every meal.

I had a lot of insecurities surrounding food and my abilities in the kitchen, so I stayed in my comfort zone until one day I just couldn't eat another salsa taco and knew something had to change.

And guess what? I quickly realized that once I knew where to find these other ingredients, they took the same exact amount of time and effort to buy at the store as my old standbys (side note: fresh herbs were new to me, so we're not talking anything crazy here). As soon as I began treating the grocery store as an adventure and not a chore, things got a whole lot easier and more delicious. No more salsa tacos.

As you start looking through the recipes in this book, I encourage you to reserve judgment and eye rolls for more serious offenses than a bean you've never heard of before. Rather than skipping past things that you don't know, pause instead. Seek out more information about them. And then go buy them and experiment. It makes this whole process so much easier (and a lot more fun) when you let down your guard and allow yourself to have more of an open mind.

And about the expensive part: it's true that some whole, plant-based ingredients cost a little more than their conventional counterparts. Whole-grain and nut flours are definitely more expensive than good ol'-fashioned white flour. But that's because you are paying for a quality product that isn't cheap to produce.

If you find that some ingredients just won't fit into your weekly food budget, save them for special occasions. You're not eating caviar at every meal, so treat your new recipes the same way. I don't want you cursing me at the checkout counter or, more important, getting too discouraged by price tags to give OPP a try.

The good news is that most of the ingredients I use and recommend in my recipes cost about the same or even less than a lot of the stuff you're probably used to buying. A half pound of nutritional yeast is far less expensive than a half pound of fancy imported cheese. And if you're asking yourself, "What the hell is nutritional yeast?"...don't worry, we'll get to that.

② **This isn't a diet book.** I'm curvy. This is something I know. I have, on occasion, worn two sports bras to the gym. I've got hips, thighs, and a booty. A woman once told me that she liked my recipes because I was a "real woman" and not super thin. It took me a second to decide that was a compliment. It was. I'm not sure if my body is designed to ever be super thin, and my food and recipes aren't designed to try to achieve that either. I create recipes with one intention in mind: to make my (and your) body feel good. A lot of you might lose weight eating more plant-based foods—I certainly did. But for many of us, even when we do drop some lbs, we'll still be rocking the double sports bra and the rest of our curves. And that's OK.

The point is, it's important to me that you know that this isn't a diet book. Don't worry, I'm not going to tell you that "it's not a diet, it's a lifestyle!" book either, because that's also not the point. This book is simply about food. OK, not just any food; it deserves a little more credit than that. It's about real food that I'm hoping is going to help give you more energy and help you feel more alive. Food that might help you begin to heal from chronic illness. Food that might inspire you to get in the kitchen and cook. And food that will leave you feeling *good* after eating it (hint: real food doesn't make you feel depressed or so bloated you look pregnant). So yes, it's pretty special stuff. But it's also not the food you'll find in a lot of diet books, the kind that makes you feel restricted or that you're missing out. I don't want you to approach my recipes with any of these emotions. I want you to eat food that you're excited about.

One of my health heroes, Dr. Mark Hyman, says, "Food is not just calories or energy. Food contains information that talks to your genes." I keep this in mind every time I make a decision about what to eat. I don't ask myself, *Will this food make me fat?* I ask, *Is this food going to whisper sweet nothings to my body/genes and make them feel good, or is it going to be like my dick ex-boyfriend and say rude things that make my body/genes feel bad?* Yes, I definitely eat the occasional French fry (or twenty). But I shoot for the feel-good foods 90 percent of the time.

Wait, did I mention this isn't a diet book? I wanted to get that in there one more time.

3 You're not perfect. Neither am I. In my dream world, does everyone eat plant-based foods at every meal? Yep. Is everyone going to actually do that? Nope. I'm OK with that. All I want is for you to try to eat at least one plant-based meal a day. The cool thing is you've got three chances to make that happen. If it's not at breakfast, lunch is right around the corner. If you still can't fit it in by lunch, you've got dinner. I also know that for a lot of you (and this is something I do secretly want to happen), one meal might turn to two, and two might turn to three. Until one day, you wake up and this thing you tried has become your new norm.

It can happen. It happened to me.

There are a lot of theories out there about the best way to start a new habit. Some people believe it's best to quit the bad stuff cold turkey and go all in on a new program. Others say it's best to ease into it. And then there's the popular theory of doing something for 21 days to rewire your brain. I think all of these approaches are right, because every single person approaches change differently. No matter what path you take, it's important to remember that nobody's perfect. You've got hundreds of meals ahead of you to figure out what works best. It doesn't have to be all or nothing; you're just shooting for one meal a day to start. And if that one meal doesn't happen, wake up the next morning and try again.

I once had a dinner meeting with a woman, and before we even got a chance to sit down at the table, she told me that she wasn't interested in eating a plant-based diet. I politely smiled and told her we were cool and I wasn't planning on asking her to eat one anyway. The funny thing is that as we ate, she drilled me with questions about my diet—why I eat the way I do, if it was hard, if I missed any of the old foods I used to eat, and if I noticed a difference in the way I felt each day. I answered all her questions and pointed out a couple times that she was bringing up my diet, not me. I had a hunch that she was actually a little interested in trying a plant-based diet. I suggested that the easiest way for people (not her, of course) to get started was with one meal a day.

Today this woman who so boldly proclaimed that she had no interest in trying a plant-based diet eats a diet primarily composed of—you guessed it—plants. She started slowly, with smoothies for breakfast, then began adding more veggies to her dinners, and then decided to cut out dairy. Now she's almost all in. I bring her up because I've come across many people like her—so afraid to change that they don't even want to try. Maybe it's a fear of missing out on favorite foods or being intimidated by learning new cooking techniques, but I think for a lot of people it comes down to not wanting to fail. Whatever the reason, they still hear a tiny (like so tiny they can barely make it out) voice inside that's telling them to try. I encourage you to listen to that voice and then tell that voice to not even think about judging you when you do.

I didn't want to change my diet. But I listened to that voice that asked, *What if this works? What if this actually makes you feel* good? *What if you can still be the same you, but feel more alive?* Thank goodness I listened. Changing how I ate was one of the hardest things I've ever done, but it's also one of my greatest accomplishments. I'm happier, nicer, and I feel pretty damn good, too. I achieved all this without being perfect and by simply taking things one meal at a time.

OPP in the Kitchen

I just took stock of my entire kitchen, and here's what I found:

1 BLENDER	1 CUPCAKE PAN
1 FOOD PROCESSOR	2 SPATULAS
1 BIG POT	2 SIEVES (FINE-MESH BOWL)
1 SMALL PAN	3 BIG SPOONS
1 BIG PAN	1 WHISK
1 SAUCEPAN	1 HANDHELD MIXER
1 CAST-IRON SKILLET	1 EACH: CHEF'S KNIFE, SERRATED KNIFE, AND PARING KNIFE (A.K.A. "THAT SMALL KNIFE")
1 PIE PAN	3 BIG BOWLS
1 WIRE RACK	1 GRATER
1 8-BY-11 BAKING DISH	1 CITRUS JUICER THING
3 BAKING SHEETS	1 ROLL OF PARCHMENT PAPER

It's not a lot. I don't have a mandoline or a fancy set of knives or rice cooker or waffle maker (although I really do want a waffle maker). Most of my friends and family have double the amount of kitchen gear that I do, and they rarely cook.

When I first started teaching myself how to cook, I think the only reason I had most of these items was because my husband, Dan, loves to cook. For the first ten years of our marriage, he was the official chef in our kitchen, and he made every meal. The few times that I attempted to help, I once famously burned a hole in the wall, and I managed to overcook (or undercook) rice every time. When he was out of town or worked late, I'd order in, fire up the microwave, or just eat a big bowl of cereal. I had zero confidence in my ability to cook. I thought it was just something you were good at or you weren't.

When I first started eating a plant-based diet, Dan was still doing a lot of the cooking. But as I started to experience the changes this new food was having on me, I became curious and excited to get into the kitchen myself. Food was helping me heal and becoming such an important part of my life that I couldn't let myself be intimidated by the kitchen anymore. Not to mention, Dan worked a lot of late nights, and all those takeout and frozen meals didn't quite fit into my new deal...so I had to suck it up and figure out meals I could make for myself.

The first meal I "cooked" on my own was a salsa taco (as mentioned, salsa tacos were my go-to meal when I first went plant-based). Granted, a ten-year-old who was allowed to hold a knife could have put this meal together. But I made salsa from scratch, dammit, and I was proud! I remember I even took a photo of it and sent it to my friend. But after a few too many salsa tacos, I knew I needed to switch it up and learn how to cook from actual recipes.

And then, the Birthday Cake Incident happened.

A few weeks after changing my diet, I went to a good friend's birthday party. When the cake came out, I panicked. I fought back tears as everyone was singing "Happy Birthday." As they started to cut the cake, I stepped outside and really started to cry. I was crying partly because I thought I couldn't stuff my face with the vanilla frosting I loved so much, but what was really making me sad was the sense of loss I felt over the food traditions that would no longer be part of my life. My stupid new diet was taking them away from me. I was sad, but I also couldn't ignore the fact that the new food I was eating was helping me heal my body. I wanted my cake and my health, too.

I decided that I needed to figure out how to cook all of my favorite foods in a new way. I started with the classics I grew up with, swapping out a few ingredients here and there to make them plant-based—pasta dishes, mashed potatoes and gravy, cookies, and pies. I practiced a lot. I failed a lot. But the more I tried, the less scary my kitchen became.

I no longer believe that cooking is something you're naturally good at or you're not. Just like a lot of things in our lives, cooking skills are acquired through practice. My recipes aren't super elaborate, and you're not going to learn some crazy-advanced chef technique that involves making foam from a vegetable. What I do want is to give you simple and delicious dishes that you feel confident preparing, that you love to eat, and that make you feel really good.

It was important to me that all of the recipes in this book be made and taste tested by someone besides me. So I enlisted the help of family, friends, readers of my website, and listeners of my podcast to test-drive all of the recipes you're about to see. They aren't professional chefs or cookbook authors—they are people who simply love food. I got such great feedback from them that I've included some of their thoughts and tips about the recipes called "Tasters Tell All" throughout this book.

If you're still thinking, *But I am really bad at cooking*—just stop. As a former wall-burning, can't-even-make-rice mess in the kitchen, I'm not going to be able to give you a pass. I know you can do this. Don't wait until you find yourself crying outside of someone else's birthday party over a piece of cake. Pick a recipe. Read it all the way through. And make it. And then make it again until you've got it right. You might surprise yourself.

2 | Pantry Essentials

There used to be a time in our house each day that my husband referred to as the "Magic Hour." The Magic Hour was when I had come home super hungry after a long day at work and couldn't figure out what to have for dinner. The frantic downward spiral would start off with me saying things like, "It takes too much time to cook!" and "Why don't we ever have groceries?!" and would eventually progress to "It's too late to order delivery!" and "Well, what do YOU want to eat?"

He was being sarcastic, of course, because this hour was the opposite of magic. It was terrible. I'm not the nicest when I'm hungry, and back then I was also in a lot of pain. Not to mention, I had zero idea what to do in the kitchen, which only deepened the spiral.

After a few epic Magic Hour meltdowns, I would plan a weekend trip to the grocery store and imagine the amaaazzzing experience it was going to be. I pictured myself floating through the aisles and getting inspired by all of the interesting ingredients that I saw. I would leave with a cart full of delicious, healthy food that would feed me for the whole week. I was going to be prepared! It was going to be awesome! But in reality, I'd get to the store, feel overwhelmed by indecision, get frustrated with myself for not making a list ahead of time, and leave nearly empty-handed (except for an apple or two).

When I shifted to eating more real food and slowly started becoming more comfortable and confident at the store and in my kitchen, I began to notice a trend in the ingredients I was consistently buying. I also noticed that these same ingredients were saving me from having Magic Hour meltdowns. If I had these ingredients, plus some fruits and veggies, I could always throw something together for dinner.

I took stock of these items and they became my Top 10 Pantry Ingredients. I made sure to have them on hand at all times. When I headed to the grocery store, I'd do a quick scan, and if one was missing, I'd make sure to replace it.

The list below isn't a comprehensive inventory of my pantry. It doesn't account for all the seasonings, sauces, and crunchy snacks I love to buy. But these pantry essentials are the very best place to start. Scoop them up at the store, get the hang of cooking with them, and then start to create your own list of essentials for your kitchen. Once you have them (plus lots of fruits and veggies), the Magic Hour might actually become...magical.

Top 10 Pantry Ingredients (+ 2)

➊ Gluten-Free Flours

Wheat flours may be the most common, but there are a lot of flours that happen to be gluten-free, which is pretty awesome. They're great to have on hand for pancakes, cookies, and to use as a thickening agent in some recipes. There are so many gluten-free flours to choose from, it seems that every time I go to the store, I find a new one to experiment with: brown rice, buckwheat (gluten-free, even though it has *wheat* in the name), almond, oat, chickpea (garbanzo bean), coconut, amaranth, millet, quinoa, teff, and masa harina flour.

Because there are so many, I chose just a handful to use consistently in my recipes: almond, chickpea (garbanzo bean), brown rice, and masa harina. All of the flours I call for are gluten-free, but if you eat gluten and want to experiment with more whole flours, spelt and barley are good places to start.

Favorite recipes using gluten-free flours: Blueberry Corn Cakes (page 60), Saag Plant-neer (page 142), Chocolate Chunk Cookies (page 190).

❷ Plant-Based Milks

Plant-based milk can be used as a direct swap for dairy milk in most recipes, as well as anywhere else you'd usually use dairy milk. I prefer buying unsweetened milk because it's more versatile and can be used for a wide variety of dishes. Almond milk and rice milk are great for everything from cereal to mashed potatoes. Coconut milk brings a rich creaminess to desserts and smoothies. Other dairy-alternative milks include hemp, cashew, pistachio, and hazelnut. Most store-bought plant-based milks are shelf-stable and don't need to be refrigerated, so you can stock up and make sure to have them on hand at all times. When purchasing nonrefrigerated milks, do an extra-good job of reading the labels carefully. Avoid those that contain an additive called carrageenan and added sweeteners. You can also make your own nut milks at home (see page 56 for a simple recipe).

Favorite recipes using milks: Nutty Banana Smoothie (page 49); Jalapeño Corn Bread (page 84); Roasted Potato, Corn, and Leek Chowder (page 128).

❸ Nuts and Seeds

Protein-packed nuts and seeds are a plant-based cooking must. Cashews are the secret to making creamy sauces. Chia can be used as a thickening agent and binder for pudding and jams. And throwing some roasted nuts or seeds in a salad adds texture and always makes it feel a bit more finished. In the pages ahead, we'll also be experimenting with making our own nut butters (which is surprisingly easy and requires only one base ingredient: nuts). I suggest stocking up on a variety of nuts—raw and unsalted whenever possible—not only for cooking, but for snack attacks, too. Just a handful can really fill you up.

There are so many nuts and seeds to explore. Most of the ones listed here are readily available at the grocery store and online. Pick something you've never tried before and start playing in the kitchen. Nuts: almonds, pistachios, pecans, walnuts, hazelnuts, Brazil, and pine. Seeds: chia, hemp, pumpkin, sesame, flax, sunflower, quinoa, and amaranth (both quinoa and amaranth are often classified as grains, but they're technically seeds).

One last note: many of us have a hard time digesting raw nuts—they can cause a bloated stomach and can make us feel heavy in the middle. The best way to avoid this is to soak them first. This neutralizes their naturally occurring enzyme inhibitors, which allows for better digestion and easier absorption of nutrients. Begin by soaking the nuts and seeds in water with a little salt for seven to twenty-four hours, then press the water out with a towel. You can eat them right away or dry them out in an oven set at the lowest temperature or in a dehydrator (this can take up to twenty-four hours). If your budget allows, you can also buy nuts and seeds that have already been soaked (or "sprouted").

Favorite recipes using nuts and seeds: Chilaquiles with Cilantro Cream (page 63), Chocolate Cashew Butter (page 75), Creamy Mushroom Lasagna (page 155).

④ Tahini

If you've ever eaten hummus or baba ganoush, chances are you've had tahini. It's a creamy paste made from sesame seeds that has a consistency similar to almond butter. And just like almond butter, it's one of the most versatile ingredients in my pantry—I use it all the time in dips, as a base for salad dressings (just add a little lemon juice, salt, and water), and even desserts. The first time you try it, you might be a little surprised by the taste. Even though it looks like almond butter, it's slightly bitter, but bitter in the best possible way! Its unique flavor and versatility make this ingredient a pantry staple.

Favorite recipes using tahini: White Bean Buffalo Hummus (page 83), Daniel Holzman's Chopped Vegetable Salad (page 115), Tahini Ball Balls (page 210).

⑤ Natural Sweeteners

These days there is a growing awareness of the dangers of sugar—especially refined sugar. Thanks in part to some large-scale public health campaigns, we know that sugar is contained in just about every processed food and beverage out there—and that Americans are overdosing on it as a result. In fact, the FDA is so concerned about our sugar consumption that shortly before this book went to press, they released new guidelines mandating that added sugars must appear in a separate line on food labels.

Sugar has been linked to a number of health problems, from obesity and diabetes to heart disease and cancer. And while added and refined sugars may be the worst culprits, let's be clear about one thing: whether natural or refined, sugar is sugar. It's definitely an ingredient to use in moderation.

But when we do want something sweet, whole, unprocessed, and natural sugars are the best options. The body processes these types of sugar differently than refined sugars, and some natural sugars even offer their own nutritional benefits. In this book, I use dates, raw honey, and maple syrup as sweeteners—I think they're the easiest to find and most versatile to cook with. Dates magically turn to caramel when blended with a little bit of salt. Maple syrup is a great replacement for refined sugar in baking. Raw honey can transform a boring bowl of oatmeal into a delicious bowl of goodness. When it comes to honey, I always recommend buying raw honey. Raw honey isn't processed or heated—which means that you'll still get all the good stuff (the vitamins and antioxidants) that is lost during the heating process. Other choices for natural sweeteners include brown rice syrup, stevia, coconut sugar, and monk fruit sweetener.

All of that said, there are a few recipes in this book that call for dark or dairy-free chocolate—and chocolate typically contains cane sugar. Yes, I know I just said natural sweeteners are best. They are. But remember what I said earlier about not being perfect? Apply that logic here.

When you do buy dark chocolate, aim for 70 percent or higher cacao. Do your best to find varieties that contain only dark chocolate with a touch of sugar, some vanilla, and any additions you love (almonds, peppermint, dried fruit, etc.). And if you can find dark chocolate without sugar, even better!

Favorite recipes using natural sweeteners: Baklava-ish Toast (page 53), Kale Avocado Salad (page 110), Honey Peppermint Cups (page 172).

⑥ Beans and Lentils

Beans and lentils are an easy source of protein for so many plant-based meals. From veggie tacos to soups and dips, beans and lentils come in super handy on busy weeknights. Bean purists will tell you to never buy canned beans because they don't taste as good as beans you've soaked and cooked yourself. And it's true, the homemade versions often do taste better than their canned counterparts. But I see no shame in grabbing a few cans of beans to throw together a chili for your family or a quickie dip for entertaining. Most times you won't know the difference. In the recipes that follow, you'll see that I do use canned beans, but you always have an option to substitute with ones you prepare at home (especially if you are one of those aforementioned bean purists).

If you do go the canned route, look for BPA-free cans and check the ingredient list to make sure there are no "flavorings," soy additives, or sugars. You just want the beans with salt or kombu (kelp) if you like it. Always make sure to drain and rinse canned beans thoroughly under cold water before using.

Personally, I always cook my own lentils, and I do simmer my own black-eyed peas—I swear, they taste so much better than the canned ones. But you do what works for you. I suggest you start your own little bean and lentil test kitchen to decide what you prefer. There are so many options to try. Beans: black, pinto, kidney, fava, great northern, white, lima, black-eyed peas, cannellini, chickpeas (garbanzos), and cranberry. Lentils: black (beluga), green (Puy and French), red, yellow, brown, mung, and split mung (these are both called "beans," but generally are classified as lentils).

In addition to using straight-up beans and lentils, you can also find some pretty delicious noodles made from them. Mung, black bean, and red lentil pastas are among my favorites and work great with veggie stir-fries or tossed with pesto sauce and veggies.

Favorite recipes using beans and lentils: Vinson Petrillo's Fresh Chickpea Spread with Crispy Black Olives (page 77), Tomato and White Bean Panzanella (page 108), Corn Cakes with Black Bean Spread (page 160).

⑦ Gluten-Free Grains

Grains are the perfect way to add heartiness to your meal. If I know I've got a busy week ahead, I'll make a batch or two to have them ready to go—some oats soaked with almond milk for breakfast or a big batch of brown rice that just needs some fresh veggies and a really great sauce. All the grains used in this book are gluten-free, but if you have a sensitivity to gluten or celiac disease, always read the label to ensure they aren't packaged at the same plant as products containing gluten.

Grains that are gluten-free include rice (brown, black, jasmine, basmati, Arborio), millet, sorghum, oats, teff, and corn. Grains that are not gluten-free but are still whole include spelt, whole wheat, farro, bulgur, and rye.

As with beans and lentils, a lot of manufacturers are making great gluten-free pastas from grains. After trying them all, I'd have to say brown rice pasta is my favorite in terms of tasting the most like the "real thing." It cooks quickly, doesn't get mushy, and has a consistency similar to the spaghetti you grew up with. Tinkyáda is my favorite brand and comes in lots of cool shapes and sizes—they even have lasagna noodles.

Just like nuts, grains can be soaked to make them more easily digestible. Some diets suggest restricting grains due to the belief that our bodies are not designed to properly digest them. This might be the case for some people, but see what works for you. If brown rice makes you bloated, try soaking it before giving it up. If it still makes you look like you're in your second trimester, move on to a different grain (or seed) and find one that your body agrees with.

Favorite recipes using whole grains: Crunchy Chunky Granola (page 54), Spicy Broccoli Rice (page 167), Pistachio Coconut Squares (page 212).

8 Coconut

It's pretty amazing how one kooky-looking plant can do so much in the kitchen. Inside that hairy little shell are tons of healthy and delicious ingredients.

Coconut milk has become a staple in plant-based cooking, not only because its rich and creamy texture makes it one of the best stand-ins for dairy milk, but also because it contains a nice serving of healthy fats. It can be used in everything from chia pudding to overnight oats to curries to whipped cream. When using it for baking and desserts, canned full fat works best (especially for whipped cream). For curries and savory dishes, you can use light—but I generally stick to full fat for most recipes because it produces a richer result and it's usually the only fat I'll be using in the dish.

Coconut water is super hydrating and rich in electrolytes. It's my go-to for smoothies, refreshing coolers, and making fruity ice pops in the summer. I also have a friend who swears that it's the perfect hangover cure. Keep that in mind for the next time you overdo it on the tequila.

Unsweetened shredded coconut and coconut flakes are incredible for plant-based baking, desserts, and even breakfast. They add texture to cookies and make a great topping for oatmeal and ice cream.

Coconut oil has become my generation's duct tape: it can do anything, and you can find a hundred ways to use it. I'm not kidding—I actually just saw an article the other day titled "101 Ways to Use Coconut Oil." It's great for roasting and sautéing vegetables or adding to smoothies, and it can be used as a substitute for butter in baking. Outside of the kitchen, it makes a pretty great skin care ingredient, too.

When you buy a jar of coconut oil, the oil will most likely be solid. But for the recipes in this book, you'll want to use it in its liquid form. Luckily, coconut oil is pretty sensitive to heat and melts quickly. Put a tiny bit in the palm of your hand, and you'll see what I mean. To turn solid coconut oil into liquid, you can melt the amount you need in a small pan or run it under hot water. In the summer months, you might not even need to melt it at all. Like I said, it's very sensitive to heat!

Favorite recipes using coconut: French Toast Sandwich with Cinnamon Cardamom Syrup (page 67), Creamy Succotash (page 102), Julia Turshen's Strawberry Granita With Coconut Whipped Cream (page 194).

⑨ Seed and Nut Butters

When I have time, I like to make my own nut butters—but let's face it, a jar of almond butter can save you when all you have in the fridge is some sliced bread or you need to whip up a last-minute dessert to bring to a dinner party. Also a spoonful slathered on a piece of celery or apple always seems to take the edge off pre-dinner hunger.

Most grocery stores offer a pretty great variety of nut and seed butters—almond butter, cashew butter, and hazelnut butter. If you're allergic to nuts, sunflower seed butter is a great alternative (and is pretty tasty even if you aren't allergic to nuts). When you're shopping, stay away from brands that include additives and sugars. Purchase varieties that list nuts and maybe some salt as the only ingredients.

You might have noticed that I didn't include peanut butter in the list above. No, it's not be-cause peanuts are actually a legume (little trivia bomb for you). I didn't include it because, like gluten, peanuts are the subject of heated nutritional debate. The anti-peanut camp says that peanuts contain a naturally occurring fungal toxin that can be carcinogenic and that peanuts contain a high percentage of omega-6 fats, which can cause inflammation. The pro-peanut camp says that as long as the peanut butter is organic and eaten in moderation, it's perfectly safe and offers a great source of protein. Personally I eat peanut butter from time to time, but 90 percent of the time, I stick with almond, cashew, and hazelnut butter. In most of my recipes, I recommend using one of these nut butters—but if you've got some natural peanut butter that will work in a pinch, do you.

Favorite recipes using seeds and nut butters: Chia Fruit Toast (page 44), Easy Red Curry Veggie Bowls (page 148), Coconut Date Pinwheels (page 185).

⑩ Veggie Broth

Homemade or store-bought, I always recommend keeping broth on hand to add flavor to a variety of dishes or use as a base for soups. You'll also notice in some recipes that I use veggie broth in place of oil to sauté vegetables. It adds a little extra flavor to your veggies, and I try to use less oil whenever I can.

When buying packaged broth, make sure to read the label and purchase the types without additives like MSG and dyes. And if you're trying to cut back on sodium, find low-sodium broth.

If you plan on making your own veggie broth, keep a little veggie scraps bag going in your fridge. All those pieces of onions, garlic, mushrooms, and green stems left on your cutting board can be thrown in a pot with water, salt, and a little kombu to make homemade broth. Freeze the broth in baggies or ice cube trays in your freezer for quick use.

Favorite recipes using veggie broth: Spicy Broccoli Rice (page 167), Roasted Cauliflower and Fennel Soup (page 126), Mashed Potato and Gravy Bowl (page 158).

PLUS...

These two ingredients were in the running for the Top 10, but for one reason or another got bumped by another ingredient. I wanted to make sure to include them, though, because they're still an integral part of my pantry, and you'll be seeing them a lot in the recipes that follow.

⑪ Nutritional Yeast

If you're new to plant-based cooking, this ingredient is probably going to be the most unusual one in the book. Before I changed my diet, I had never even heard of it. But now it's always stocked in my pantry.

Nutritional yeast is a deactivated yeast that looks a lot like fish food. It has a deep yellow hue and is sold in large flakes or in a powdered form. Don't be scared—it really is the best way to add a salty, cheeselike vibe to pastas, soups, and popcorn. And I don't know about you, but I never want to say goodbye to cheese vibes.

Many nutritional yeast brands fortify their flakes with B12, a critical vitamin for healthy cells and brain function. It's the one vitamin that you're not going to be able to get from plants. It can only be found in animal products, so I like to buy the fortified brand to get all the extra B12 I can. If you decide to go mostly or go all in on plant-based eating, your nutritional yeast won't be enough, and you'll need to take a B12 supplement. Regardless of your diet, I suggest getting your B12 levels tested next time you see your doctor. Deficiency in B12 can lead to fatigue, moodiness, depression, and other serious issues.

My favorite brand of nutritional yeast is Kal; it's non-GMO and has the extra bonus shot of B12 added.

Favorite recipes using nutritional yeast: Creamy Grits with Avocado and Hot Sauce (page 62), Herb Fries (page 97), Roasted Asparagus and Tomato Pasta (page 136).

⑫ Tamari

OK, this might be the other ingredient you aren't familiar with—but this one is super easy to explain: Tamari is gluten-free soy sauce. Soy sauce has gluten?! Yes, I was surprised, too. But almost all commercial soy sauces contain wheat, and a lot of them also contain caramel coloring and corn syrup.

Tamari can be used exactly the same as you would traditional soy sauce and in new ways that aren't as traditional. I love using it to add an extra layer of flavor to curry sauces, and when I'm sautéing mushrooms, I always add a splash to kick up the umami factor.

My favorite brand of tamari is San-J. Not only is it delicious, but you can find it at most grocery stores, they make an organic option, and the ingredient list is short and sweet (water, organic soybeans, salt, organic alcohol to preserve freshness).

If you have an allergy to soy or do not include it in your diet, coconut aminos are a great substitute for tamari.

Favorite recipes using tamari: Mexican Fried Rice Nachos (page 141), Creamy Butternut Squash and Lentil Tacos (page 143), Thai Coconut Soup (page 130).

Navigating the Store

Over the years, I've helped a lot of friends and family members find their One Part Plant groove. When they tell me they're ready to eat more plants, I get excited and send them recipes, lend them my favorite cookbooks, share my pantry essentials, and even host little powwows to address all their burning plant-based questions. They leave armed with everything they need know, and they're excited to get started.

And then they go to the grocery store. Alone.

When they hit the store for the first time, my phone starts buzzing. "Where do you find tahini? I've looked everywhere!" "No one at this store has ever heard of tamari!" and "Why are there so many kinds of lentils? That's a rhetorical question. But really, why are there so many kinds of lentils?"

I've been there. I was just as confused about where to find plant-based staples at the beginning of my OPP journey. But I want to make this transition as easy as possible for you, so I've compiled a handy little grocery store guide to get you started.

When you simply can't find an item at your local store, I recommend buying it online. I do that a lot. There are a lot of great retailers that sell plant-based essentials—Vitacost.com, Thrivemarket.com, and Woodlandfoods.com are three of my favorites—and of course Amazon will pretty much always have everything you're looking for. You can also check out the SHOP section of my site to see my favorite brands and pick up some things there.

Every retailer is a little different in terms of how they stock their aisles, but the following cheat sheet is generally pretty accurate.

Finding Your Pantry Essentials: A Grocery Store Map

1 **Gluten-Free Flours:** You can either find them in the baking aisle with the rest of the flours or in a specialty aisle that carries gluten- and dairy-free products. This aisle is most commonly called "alternative," "natural," or "special diets."

2 **Plant-Based Milks:** Plant-based milks are usually found in the cereal aisle, unrefrigerated, although I've seen them popping up more and more in the dairy case, too. My favorite brand of almond milk is Califia (it's carrageenan-free) and it can be found next to the dairy milk in most stores.

③ **Nuts and Seeds:** The bulk aisle is the best place to go for nuts and seeds because you're able to select exactly what you need, and oftentimes the value is better. Some stores devote a whole section to nuts, usually in the snack aisle. Just be sure to read the labels carefully: you want to buy raw, unsalted nuts. Skip any that contain sweeteners, spices, or additives.

④ **Tahini:** Tahini can usually be found in the peanut butter section with the other seed and nut butters. You'll most likely spot it on the bottom shelf. If it's not there, look for it in the "international" aisle. If you have access to a Middle Eastern market, you'll have no problem finding it there. There are also a handful of boutique and small-batch tahini brands—Soom and Seed + Mill are two to check out. Sometimes they are a little pricier than the kind you'll find at the grocery store, but worth the splurge if you start becoming a tahiniaholic and want to drizzle it on everything.

⑤ **Natural Sweeteners:** Maple syrup and raw honey are almost always in the baking aisle. Another great place to find them—usually locally sourced versions—is at farmers' markets. Unlike the grocery store brands, small-batch versions of honey might not be labeled as "raw," but they usually are—just ask to be sure.

Dates are tricky to find sometimes. If your store has a bulk foods section, head there first. If there are no bulk bins, you can often find dates in an aisle with other dried fruits and nuts. You might also find them hiding out in the produce section—at my local grocery store, they are sitting in a box above the bananas. I've even seen them in the refrigerated section with the cut/prepared fruit.

Buy dates that are fresh, plump, and soft. They should be a little shiny looking.

If you're not able to find super soft and shiny dates, you can always soak them in hot water before using them in recipes.

⑥ **Beans and Lentils:** Just like nuts, I recommend buying dried beans and lentils by weight in the bulk foods section. If your store doesn't have a bulk section, you can usually find bags of dried beans and lentils in the rice aisle. If you're buying canned beans, they're usually stocked with the canned veggies.

7 **Gluten-Free Grains:** The bulk foods area usually has a wide selection of grains such as quinoa, amaranth, and brown rice. If bulk isn't an option, you can find a nice variety of packaged grains in the rice aisle.

8 **Coconut:** Canned coconut milk is usually located in the "international" or "Asian" section of the store. Occasionally, you may find it in the baking section. Coconut oil is most likely shelved with all the other oils, but it, too, can sometimes be found in the baking section (not to be confused with coconut butter). Coconut flakes/shreds are usually available prepackaged in the baking section, but check out the bulk bins, too—the prices may even be better. Either way, always opt for unsweetened coconut.

9 **Seed and Nut Butters:** These can be found in the peanut butter aisle or sometimes in the "special diets" or "natural foods" aisle. Some grocery stores also have the option to grind your own nut butter, which is a great choice—you know there is nothing in it but the nuts themselves.

10 **Veggie Broth:** Broth—both in cartons and cans—is usually located in the soup aisle. Look for organic broths and be sure to scan the label for additives like MSG, high-fructose corn syrup, and autolyzed yeast extract.

11 **Nutritional Yeast:** You can often find nutritional yeast in the "special diets" or "natural" section or in the vitamin aisle. If you find it in the vitamin section, you might have to commit to a large tub, which might seem a little pricey, but it will last you a very long time. Some grocers may not carry it at all, but you can easily find nutritional yeast at a health food store or online.

12 **Tamari:** Tamari can be found with the other soy sauces in the "international" or "Asian" aisle.

Herbs and Spices: The Other Pantry Staples

If you're new to cooking (plant-based or not), salt and pepper might be the only seasonings in your pantry. That's OK! You have two of the most important ones, and we'll start building from there. I'm not going to ask you to go out and buy one of those crazy twenty-four-piece spice sets (unless you want to). I just want you to get some basics as you work your way through these recipes—cinnamon, cumin, chili powder, red pepper flakes, thyme, and turmeric are a great place to start. When you're cooking with plants, herbs and spices really bring everything together.

If you have been cooking for a while, do me a favor—head over to your spice rack and take stock of what you've got. If you're rocking cinnamon that you've had since college, it's time to replace it (unless you graduated a few months ago, in which case, way to go!). Using spices and herbs past their expiration date won't hurt you, but it also won't add a lot of flavor to your food. Some spice experts say that you should replace your spices every six months, and others say two years is fine. I fall somewhere right in the middle—I try not to hold on to spices for longer than a year or so. No matter when you decide to replace them, do a quick inventory before your next trip to the grocery store. Check the expiration or the "best by" dates and replace them as needed. You want your spices and herbs to be as potent as possible. Your taste buds will thank you.

Salt to Taste and Some Other Important Notes on Seasoning

My taste buds have changed dramatically since I started eating a plant-based diet. For all you former smokers out there, you know exactly what I'm talking about. When you quit smoking, your once-dulled senses of smell and taste become sharper and more perceptive. Suddenly food has more intense flavor. When I cut out all the processed foods and candy, I had a similar awakening. Everything I ate tasted different. Whole foods (read: vegetables) that I was never excited about were quickly becoming my favorites. They actually tasted *good*. And processed foods—with tons of sweeteners and salt—suddenly tasted *not* so good.

In fact, I developed some pretty major salt issues. Before I went plant-based, I couldn't get enough salt. Now if someone overdoes it just a little, I'm a Salt-Sensitive Sally. It's a known fact in my house that I'm a serial underseasoner. To my friends and family, there's never enough salt in the dishes I make, when to me, they taste just right. I've learned not to take it personally when someone adds a hearty pinch of salt to something I've cooked for them. Everyone's taste buds are different when it comes to salt.

Because of this, I've left the salt quantities open in most of my recipes so that you can salt it up just the way you like it. When it comes to baking, though, I've given you exact instructions and wouldn't suggest deviating from those.

Along the same lines, I've also left the measurements for citrus and vinegar open, as everyone's preferences for acid or sourness differ, too. I suggest starting with a little at a time, tasting, and adding more as you go.

If you're a new cook, don't let the lack of specific measurements freak you out. When I first started cooking, I would follow recipes to a T, and lots of times, I just didn't like the way they turned out. It wasn't because the recipes were flawed—it was about my palate and what tastes good to me. If you're going to spend the time to make one of my recipes, I want you to love the results. Add more red pepper flakes if you want some extra heat or add another half of a lemon if you need more acid. Don't be afraid to experiment in the kitchen. Take liberties with my recipes and figure out what tastes best to you.

What Kind of Salt Should I Use?

———

You may notice that any time you see me call for salt in this book, I'm using sea salt (Celtic sea salt is my favorite). I highly recommend investing in a good-quality sea salt and ditching the traditional table salt that most of us grew up with. Why? Well, for starters, it tastes better. It's richer and it makes dishes more flavorful. Second, it's the more whole and natural option, and it contains trace minerals that are good for our bodies. Regular table salt is processed and oftentimes contains chemicals or additives that help prevent it from caking. If you're willing to spend a little more on one pantry staple, I would make salt the one. A good-quality sea salt really will make a difference in your cooking.

Label Reading 101

———

I'm a pretty hardcore food label reader these days. But only a few years ago, the concept was foreign to me. I'd never read a single label—with the exception of scanning the calorie and fat grams. *There's no fat in this giant bag of gummy worms? AWESOME. I can eat the whole thing!* What I wasn't seeing was that those gummy worms were full of sugar, artificial coloring, and ingredients that I couldn't even pronounce. Ingredients that were making me sick.

I don't want you to become an OCD label reader who's scared to buy anything that's not perfect—but I do think it's really, really important to read the ingredients label on all packaged foods, especially since the words used on the front of a package can often be misleading.

Here's what to look for:

1. It's a good first step to see if the food in question is actually the food it is marketed to be. So many foods on grocery store shelves are imitations of the real thing. For example, let's look at one of the most popular brands of what we consider "maple syrup." It's one that most Americans grew up with and still eat today. It doesn't even contain any actual maple syrup! Here's the ingredient list: high-fructose

corn syrup, corn syrup, water, salt, cellulose gum, molasses, potassium sorbate (preservative), sodium hexametaphosphate, citric acid, caramel color, natural and artificial flavors. It's absolutely insane. An ingredient list for maple syrup should consist of two words: *maple* and *syrup*.

2 Ditch the sugar. OK, before you call me out, I know maple syrup is sugar. When I say to ditch sugar, I'm referring to all of the processed sugars that are added to everything from pasta sauces to boxed teas. Once you start looking, you're going to be shocked by how often sugar turns up as an ingredient in your food. Also be warned that sugar goes by a lot of different names. These are most common: sucrose, high-fructose corn syrup, dextrose, and maltose.

3 Look for real foods with names you actually recognize. Highly processed ingredients and chemicals aren't real food, and it's crazy that food companies are passing them off as if they are. They can cause a host of problems for the body, some of which we might not yet be aware of. Outside the US, many of these ingredients are banned, but in the US food manufacturers haven't stopped using these dangerous ingredients.

Avoid buying any packaged foods that contain the most common culprits: monosodium glutamate (MSG), artificial sweeteners (aspartame, a.k.a. NutriSweet), high-fructose corn syrup, and food dyes (ingredients that start with *red, blue,* and *yellow,* and are followed by numbers are not good).

Bottom line: if you're unsure about an ingredient, look it up. The Environmental Working Group (EWG) has an incredible resource on their website called Food Scores (ewg.org/foodscores) where you can search more than eighty thousand foods and get a safety rating in seconds. It's an invaluable guide for beginners and even for those who think they know it all.

3 | FAQs

I love Frequently Asked Question pages so much that I really wanted to add one to my book—and my editor even let me put it in the front! But this isn't just about me living out my FAQ fantasy—I really wanted to address the questions I had when I changed my diet, which are also generally the ones that I get asked most by my website readers and podcast listeners. If you have questions I don't answer here, check out www.jessicamurnane.com, because I've probably addressed some of them there. And I'll be updating the site as new questions come in. I mean, I really do love a good FAQ.

Does All My Food Have to Be Organic?

In a dream world, it would be amazing if everyone could buy organic versions of every food. But the reality is that organic produce and products are not always widely available, and when they are, it might not be in your budget to buy them. Just do your best and try to spend your organic food dollars where they matter most.

Every year, the Environmental Working Group (EWG) publishes a list of the fruits and vegetables that have the smallest amount of pesticide residue (Clean Fifteen) and the ones with the most (Dirty Dozen). I use this guide to help me decide what I'll buy organic every time I go grocery shopping—you can actually print a copy of these lists from their website, ewg.org.

It's also important to keep in mind that when you're shopping at a farmers' market, many of the farms have not gone through the process to get certified as organic, but that doesn't mean that they don't employ organic farming practices. So, if you don't see that certification on their sign, don't pass them up. Just ask for more information, and they're usually happy to share.

For years people told me that organic food tasted better, and for years I didn't believe it. I didn't want to have to pay any more at the grocery store than I already did. But guess what? They were right...organic produce really does taste better, and most research says it's better for our bodies, too. I've made a lot of changes at the store to enable me to buy as much organic as possible. The biggest is using EWG's list, and another big one is taking the money from that trashy magazine I was going to buy at the checkout counter and investing in organic strawberries instead.

Can I Drink Alcohol?

We're all adults here, and we all know the effects of alcohol on our minds and bodies. So I'll leave this choice up to you. If you're unsure of what to do, my advice is to really think about how alcohol makes you feel. Next time you're offered a drink, take a moment to ask yourself these questions: Will this make me feel shitty in the morning? Will this make me feel bloated? Do I feel good when I drink? You know the answers to those questions better than I do.

What About Oil?

A lot of plant-based eaters and doctors recommend excluding all oils from your diet. I can understand their reasoning. It's hard to argue with the fact that oils are high in fat and some oils are not the best for specific health issues. But this is not an oil-free book—we use it in moderation. Remember, we're looking at changing just one meal a day with some simple plant-based swaps. One step at time. The good news is if you do decide to go oil-free down the road (or already are), you'll still be able to eat most of the recipes in this book.

When you do cook with oil, be selective. Stick with high-quality olive, coconut, and grape seed oil (those are the oils I use in my recipes).

What does "high-quality olive oil" mean? I asked Maia Hirschbein, an oleologist (that's the name for an oil expert!) with California Olive Ranch about how to buy the best olive oil. Here are her top tips:

- Look for *extra-virgin* on the label; extra-virgin olive oil tastes better, is purer, and provides the most health benefits. It also has a high smoke point, so it can be used for all types of cooking and food preparation. Use it for everything from sautéing and roasting to baking and even frying.
- Avoid meaningless marketing terms like *light* or *extra light. Pure olive oil* is also misleading, and means the oil has been partially refined, so avoid it.
- When choosing a bottle from the shelf, look for dark glass or tins and turn the bottle around to check for a harvest date—it should be within the last year. Also, look for a single place of origin and avoid long lists of countries.
- Once you buy a great bottle of olive oil, use it QUICKLY. Olive oil is perishable, so you want to use it within a couple months after opening it. Store extra-virgin olive oil in a dark cool place to make it last longer.

With that said, it's easy to overdo it with the oil. It's an automatic reflex to reach for the olive oil as soon as we get the pan out to cook veggies. You don't have to stop using it; just start to become more mindful of how much you use. In this book, you'll see that in many recipes, you're given the option to use veggie broth instead of oil to sauté vegetables. This is how I cook a lot of my veggies at home.

Is It Bad to Use Frozen Fruits and Vegetables?

Not at all! I buy frozen fruit a lot, especially when berries aren't in season. The great thing about frozen fruits and veggies is that they are picked when ripe and then usually frozen right away, preserving all of their natural nutrients and flavor.

What About Eggs?

You can find a hundred articles that say that eggs are evil, and you can find another hundred that say they are great for you. Personally, I don't eat them—I don't digest them very well. If you're thinking that your stomach might not be a fan either, the best way to find out is to get the best-quality eggs you can find and eat them all by themselves. If you add butter, cheese, bread, or bacon and have a stomachache, you're going to have a hard time determining if the eggs are the culprit. Do your own research and most importantly, see how your body feels when you eat them. If you decide to eat eggs, buy free-range and organic whenever possible.

Should I Eat Plant-Based All the Time?

I used to roll my eyes at the phrase "listen to your body." I didn't get it. What exactly did it mean? How am I supposed to listen to my body? It was such an abstract concept that I couldn't figure out how it made sense for me. But when it comes to this decision, it's the best advice I can give you.

After you've been eating real foods for a while, you will notice changes in your body. And when you eat some not-so-real foods, your body will let you know right away whether it likes them or not. When I experienced this phenomenon firsthand, I finally understood the whole "listening to your body" thing. It really does tell you what it likes and what it doesn't like if you take the time to listen.

So, how do you listen? Pay attention to the way your body responds to different foods. After you eat something, do you feel tired or sluggish? Gassy or bloated? Do you have really smelly poops or you're not able to poop at all? Does your skin break out? Do other weird things happen that I haven't listed here? These reactions are how your body is trying to communicate with you. These are the things that you're supposed to be listening to.

Your body doesn't communicate via some angelic inner voice that sounds like Adele telling you the crap food you're about to eat might not make you feel enlightened today. No. It's the actual stomach cramps and constipation screaming at you as you sit in the bathroom way too long. Your body will tell you exactly how it feels.

Listening is one thing. Changing is another. It takes time. Be patient. Listen closely. Do your best, and eventually you and your body will be like old friends talking up a storm.

Can I Feed My Family a Plant-Based Diet?

I'm lucky on this front. My husband is naturally a healthy eater, and my son is a little plant-based machine—a lot of recipes in this book were inspired by him. As soon as six months hit and his pediatrician said it was cool for him to start eating solids, I started him on a whole-foods, plant-based diet. It took me thirty-three years to like green juice, and it took him one minute. He's still a toddler, so I get to decide what he eats every day. But I know it won't be that way forever. When he's old enough to buy his own food and make his own decisions, we'll see what happens. It will be his choice. For now, under our roof, it's all the plants he can eat. And that kid eats a lot of plants.

I know that not everyone has a house full of plant-based eaters, though, and this can be one of the biggest challenges when you start eating OPP. If you're a parent, you might not have the time (or desire) to make two different meals for yourself and your family. If your family is resistant to "healthy" foods, start out slow with meals that are similar to what they already enjoy.

Throughout this book, I'll call out the recipes I think are good gateway meals to plant-based eating for kids and adults. Surprisingly, it can sometimes be the adults who put up the most resistance to trying new foods! I've also found that when you include your significant other/family/extended family in meal prep, they become more open to trying new things. They feel a sense of pride in the meal they've helped to create, and they're more excited to sit down and eat it.

Remember, you don't need to go from zero to kale salads in one day. Make a pasta dish or soup that's already in their comfort zone. No need to make a big announcement that it's plant-based—serve it up like you would any other dish, and take breakfast, lunch, and dinner one meal at a time.

4 | Morning

ORANGE BASIL SHOT

CHIA FRUIT TOAST

ALMOND CHERRY MUFFINS

SUUTEI TSAI (MILK TEA)

NUTTY BANANA SMOOTHIE

JOHNNIE COLLINS'S COCONUT YOGURT WITH MANGO AND PAPAYA

PINEAPPLE MINT GREEN SMOOTHIE

BAKLAVA-ISH TOAST

CRUNCHY CHUNKY GRANOLA

OWEN + ALCHEMY'S UNSWEETENED ALMOND MILK

SPICY TAHINI AVOCADO TOAST

CREAMY PEACH PORRIDGE

BLUEBERRY CORN CAKES

CREAMY GRITS WITH AVOCADO AND HOT SAUCE

CHILAQUILES WITH CILANTRO CREAM

OVERNIGHT CHIA OATS

FRENCH TOAST SANDWICH WITH CINNAMON CARDAMOM SYRUP

BREAKFAST POTATO BOWL

Orange Basil Shot

MAKES 1 SERVING

Pantry Essential: **NATURAL SWEETENER**

As soon as I feel a cold coming on—or wake up just not feeling my absolute best—I whip up this shot, and I swear, my eyes pop open and I'm brought back to life. A holistic guru would tell you about all the good stuff happening here, how it's immune-boosting and full of great antioxidants. And all of that is true. But I also just think it tastes really good. Think of it as the best-tasting medicine ever. Ginger and cayenne can be a strong duo—a little goes a long way—so I've left the measurements pretty open here. Play around with them and see what you like best.

Juice of 1 orange

½ teaspoon raw honey

Piece of fresh ginger, peeled (I use about 1 inch)

3 large basil leaves

Cayenne pepper (start with a tiny dash and go from there)

Place all the ingredients in a high-speed blender and blend until the mixture turns smooth and green. Add more cayenne or ginger if needed; blend again. Drink up!

KITCHEN NOTES: If you have a juicer, you can peel the orange and juice it along with the ginger and basil, then stir in the cayenne and honey at the end. The shot will not turn green, but it will have a pretty, burnt-orange-sunset hue.

TASTERS TELL ALL...

"I am going to be honest and say when I smelled this shot, I was almost mad at you for making me taste it...but I loved it and now make it all the time!"

Chia Fruit Toast

MAKES 1 SERVING

Pantry Essential: **NUT BUTTER**

This is my favorite I-don't-have-time-for-breakfast breakfast: 1. Toast bread while showering. 2. Slather on nut butter with one hand while checking email. 3. Throw on berries and chia Jackson Pollock–style. 4. Put toast on paper towel and eat while walking out the door. Yes, if you have time to sit down and eat this mindfully, that's cool. But we can't always make that happen every day, and this is the perfect breakfast for one of those days.

1 tablespoon natural nut butter

1 piece gluten-free, sprouted, or bread of your choice, toasted

Handful of your favorite berries

1 teaspoon chia seeds

Spread the nut butter onto the bread. Toss on the berries. Sprinkle with chia.

NEXT LEVEL: Add some hemp for extra protein and nuttiness.

Almond Cherry Muffins

MAKES 10 MUFFINS

Pantry Essentials: **GLUTEN-FREE FLOUR, PLANT-BASED MILK, NATURAL SWEETENER, COCONUT**

My husband and I eloped in Jamaica. I've never had any regrets about not having a traditional wedding or making it a big to-do. But if you forced me to change something, I would have had an awesome wedding cake. After our little ceremony, we did eat a couple slices of Jamaican rum cake, but I'm not sure I'd describe it as "awesome." My dream cake would have been a giant tower of almond cake with big pieces of cherries throughout. Hold the frosting. These muffins are a mini version of that dream cake. They aren't super rich or dense, so it's perfectly reasonable to eat them for breakfast.

1 cup unsweetened almond milk

1 tablespoon apple cider vinegar

1 tablespoon flax meal

3 tablespoons water

1 cup chickpea (garbanzo) flour

½ cup brown rice flour

1 teaspoon baking powder

½ teaspoon baking soda

½ teaspoon sea salt

½ cup cherries, pitted and cut in half, plus extra for garnish (I use thawed frozen dark cherries)

¼ cup real maple syrup

1 teaspoon vanilla extract

1½ teaspoons almond extract

¼ cup coconut oil, melted

Slivered or crushed almonds (optional)

Preheat the oven to 350 degrees. Line a muffin pan with 10 muffin liners.

In a large bowl, combine the almond milk and apple cider vinegar. In a small glass or bowl, make a flax egg: mix the flax meal and water together. Set both the milk mixture and the flax egg to the side and let sit for at least 10 minutes.

In a medium bowl, whisk together the flours, baking powder, baking soda, and salt. Toss the cherries into the flour mixture and make sure they are coated with flour.

Add the maple syrup, flax egg, and vanilla and almond extracts to the large bowl with the almond milk mixture.

Begin to combine the flour and cherry mix into the bowl of liquids a little at a time, stirring as you go. Do your best to not overstir to keep the cherries whole. When the mixture is combined, pour in the coconut oil and give it another stir.

Fill each muffin liner with ¼ cup batter. Garnish the top of each one with a cherry half and, if you like, some slivered or crushed almonds to fancy them up. Bake for 12 to 15 minutes or until a fork or toothpick inserted in the center comes out clean. Cool the muffins on a wire rack (if you have one) before serving. Store them in an airtight container for up to a few days.

Suutei Tsai (Milk Tea)

MAKES 3-4 SERVINGS

Pantry Essential: **PLANT-BASED MILK**

My son, Sid, is half-Mongolian. Because that half doesn't come from me, I wanted to make sure to educate myself by researching his heritage and include some Mongolian traditions in our home. And of course, I started with the food.

What I learned was that because of Mongolia's location and climate, meat and dairy make up most of the region's diet. We're talking lots of meat and dairy. And meat and dairy recipes that I couldn't quite figure out how to adapt and make plant-based...until I found this tea!

Traditionally suutei tsai is made with dairy milk, but almond milk is an easy swap.

The coolest part about this tea is the salt. Yes, salt. Salted tea might be a little shocking to your palate at first, but after you get the amount just right, it's hard to go back to regular ol' tea. I left the salt quantity pretty open (in Mongolia they use a lot). Play around with it and see what you like.

3 cups water

3 cups unsweetened almond or rice milk

2 tea bags green or black tea, string and tags removed

½–1 teaspoon sea salt

In a medium pot, bring the water, milk, tea, and ½ teaspoon salt to a boil over high heat. Reduce the heat and simmer for 5 minutes. Remove the tea bags with a spoon. Add more salt if needed. Serve.

KITCHEN NOTES: Toasted millet is oftentimes added to suutei tsai. If you want to add it, toast ¼ to ⅓ cup millet with a little coconut oil in a hot pan and then add it to your simmering tea. Let the tea simmer for an extra 10 minutes, or until the millet has softened.

TASTERS TELL ALL...

"I chilled the leftover milk tea and used it to make overnight oats (see page 66). I added some sweetener, ground chia seeds, cinnamon, and almond butter, and it was delicious."

Nutty Banana Smoothie

MAKES 1 SERVING

Pantry Essentials: **PLANT-BASED MILK, NUT BUTTER**

For the longest time, I didn't like smoothies. More specifically, I didn't like smoothies that I made at home. The texture was too chunky, and they just didn't taste as good as the ones I bought at my favorite juice shop. But, why? I was using the EXACT same ingredients. But then I realized my mistake: I wasn't blending long enough. Because I didn't have the super-fancy industrial strength blender my juice shop did, my little blender needed more time to do its thing. This was the first smoothie I made at home that I actually liked. Just remember, every blender is different, so it's OK if it takes a little longer to achieve a silky-smooth, juice-shop-quality drink. Patience = delicious smoothies.

2 big handfuls spinach or 2 large kale leaves, washed and destemmed

1 cup unsweetened almond or rice milk, plus more if needed

1 banana, peeled, cut into 4 chunks, and frozen

1 tablespoon nut butter (I prefer almond)

Dash of cinnamon

Place the greens and milk in a high-speed blender and blend until the mixture turns green and smooth. This might take a couple minutes, depending on the power of your blender—especially if you're using kale. Add the rest of the ingredients and blend until they are all combined. Add more milk if needed.

NEXT LEVEL: Add a scoop of maca powder for an extra energy boost.

Johnnie Collins's Coconut Yogurt with Mango and Papaya

MAKES 4 SERVINGS

Pantry Essentials: **NUTS, SEEDS, COCONUT**

As soon as I watched a video of Chef Johnnie Collins talking about food, I knew I wanted to ask him to contribute a recipe to this book. Not because he's the head chef at the super-stylish Store Kitchen in London and Berlin, or because he has really great hair (he does). I wanted him because of his approach to food: he keeps it as simple as possible and lets the ingredients speak for themselves. No fancy, frilly chef tricks—just really beautiful food.

Johnnie says that this dish was inspired by those rare occasions he gets to eat breakfast outside in the sunshine. He loves the slow release of energy and nutrients this salad provides to get you going for the day. When plums and nectarines are in season, he says they're a great substitute for the mango and papaya.

2 tablespoons chia seeds

2 tablespoons golden flaxseeds

½ cup water

2 ripe mangos, skin and pits removed, cut into strips

2 ripe papayas, skin and seeds removed, cut into strips

2 limes

2–3 cups coconut yogurt (homemade or store-bought)

2½ tablespoons crushed Brazil nuts

1½ tablespoons shelled hemp seeds

In a small bowl, mix the chia and flaxseeds with the water and let the mixture soak for 30 minutes, stirring a couple times. Zest and juice one of the limes; set aside. Slice away the peel and pith of the second lime, cut out the segments, chop them, and set them aside.

Toss the cut mango and papaya in ¾ of the lime juice and layer the pieces on the bottom of a wide, shallow bowl.

Scatter half of the nuts, chia and flaxseed mixture, and hemp seeds over the fruit and toss to combine. This will give crunch to the fruit.

Mix the remaining lime juice with the coconut yogurt to loosen it a little and then spoon it over the center of the fruit. Flatten the yogurt a little, but don't cover the fruit all the way. You still want to be able to see the color of the fruit.

Scatter the remaining nuts and seeds over the top and finish with a scattering of lime segments for juiciness and lime zest for color.

Pineapple Mint Green Smoothie

MAKES 1 SERVING

Pantry Essential: **COCONUT**

If you're new to eating greens (no judgment here—I didn't like them until I was well into my thirties)—this is a great starter smoothie. It's sweet and refreshing, and it doesn't have an overly "green" flavor. You can thank the pineapple and mint for making that happen. If you're a smoothie pro and greens are your thing, just add another cup of spinach or go wild with some more kale or chard.

1 packed cup greens such as spinach or kale

1 cup unsweetened coconut water, plus more if needed

1 cup pineapple chunks, frozen

5–6 mint leaves

1 lime

Place the greens and coconut water in a high-speed blender and blend until the liquid turns green and smooth. This might take a couple minutes, depending on the power of your blender. Add the pineapple and mint, and blend until smooth. Add more coconut water if you need to. Squeeze in half of the lime, taste, and add the other half if you want it. Pour the smoothie into a glass and drink up.

KITCHEN NOTES: This definitely has more of a juice consistency than a traditional smoothie consistency. Because of that, it might separate as it sits. If it does, just give it a stir, and you're back in business.

Baklava-ish Toast

MAKES ENOUGH FOR 4-5 PIECES OF TOAST

Pantry Essentials: **NUTS, NATURAL SWEETENER**

After college, I worked at a Persian restaurant (shout out to Reza's), and my husband worked at a Greek restaurant (no shout out) serving tables. Needless to say, there was a lot of baklava in our lives that year. I have really great memories of that time and wanted to re-create something baklava-ish that worked for my plant-based diet. I ditched the buttery dough and a lot of the sugar that you'll traditionally find in these sweets, but kept the star of the show: the nutty cinnamon center. It's perfect for a sweet breakfast treat.

1 cup raw walnuts or pistachios (or a combo)

1 tablespoon raw honey

2 tablespoons real maple syrup

1 teaspoon cinnamon

Pinch of sea salt (optional)

¼ teaspoon fresh lemon juice

Sprouted or gluten-free bread

In a food processor fitted with the S blade, process the nuts, honey, maple syrup, cinnamon, and (if you're using it) salt until almost smooth. Add the lemon juice and pulse a few more times. You can continue blending to create a smooth paste or leave it a bit chunky (I prefer chunky).

Now you have two options: spread the mixture on a piece of toasted bread, or spread it on the bread and *then* toast it in the oven. With the oven option, the spread will bubble up a bit and seep a little into the bread. It's really delicious both ways, but if I've got an extra couple minutes, I always go for option two.

Keep the spread stored in a sealed container in the fridge for up to a week.

Crunchy Chunky Granola

MAKES 4-6 SERVINGS

Pantry Essentials: **NUTS, GRAINS, COCONUT, NATURAL SWEETENER**

It was the Nature Valley Bar that started my love affair with granola. They were so crunchy they'd nearly break your teeth, but it didn't matter because they were the perfect combination of salty and sweet (and came two to a pack!). I wanted my little Sid to experience the joy of salty and sweet granola, but with way less sugar (and I also didn't want to break the few teeth he had). This is the recipe I came up with. He eats it with a bowl of rice milk as a breakfast treat and I love using it as a topping for smoothie bowls.

1 cup raw walnuts

1 cup rolled oats

¼ teaspoon sea salt

¼ cup unsweetened flaked or shredded coconut

¼ cup real maple syrup

2 teaspoons vanilla extract

¼ cup coconut oil, melted

TASTERS TELL ALL...

"I used a blender instead of a food processor because that's the appliance I had, and it worked great. My family are huge fans of granola, and we've tried a lot, and this recipe was their favorite by far!"

Preheat the oven to 350 degrees and line a rimmed baking sheet with parchment paper.

In a food processor, pulse the walnuts until they are broken up, but not to a fine meal—you still want chunks. Add the oats and salt and pulse 10 to 15 times to break up the oats a bit; again, you want to make sure a lot of the oats are still intact.

Transfer the oat mixture into a medium bowl and stir in the coconut, maple syrup, and vanilla until combined. Add the coconut oil and give it another couple of stirs.

Press the mixture onto the prepared baking sheet. You want to make sure to spread it as evenly as you can, keeping the mixture together and not creating big holes where you see the parchment showing through (this will create the chunkiness).

Bake for 12 to 15 minutes, until the edges are slightly browned. Remove the pan from the oven and let it cool for at least 15 minutes. Don't touch it!

After the 15 minutes are up, break up the granola with your hands into whatever size chunks you love. Store it in an airtight container for two to three weeks.

Making Your Own Nut Milks

Here's the thing: most of the time I don't make my own milk. I admitted this to a cheffy friend recently, and she was surprised (and maybe a little judgy). "But it's so easy!" she protested. "How could you not!?" Well, the truth is I just don't feel like it most of the time. And between you and me, the cleanup is not so fun.

Plus, with all the smoothies, cereal, and baking, we go through a lot of nut milk in our house, and if I were making all of our milk, I'd need to whip up a new batch every other day. So I usually just pick it up from the store. I always look for the brands without sugar and weird additives, like carrageenan, which some studies have suggested can wreak havoc on the gut (see page 18 for tips on purchasing nut milk).

But my friend is right—making nut milk is pretty easy, and I'm probably just being a baby when it comes to the cleanup. Making your own is the best way to ensure you're not consuming added chemicals, and it feels pretty rewarding when you look at the big bottle of homemade milk sitting in your fridge. Not to mention, it tastes better and richer than the store-bought stuff, and you can have fun by mixing lots of different nuts and spices to get flavors and combinations you won't be able to find at the store. OK, fine. I'll start making it more often.

Since I'm committing to making my own milk more often, I'm hoping you'll be willing to give it a try, too. To educate us both on the proper technique, I went to the best nut milk makers I know, Owen + Alchemy, for guidance.

Here are their tips for making unsweetened almond milk at home:

· Soak the nuts in the fridge overnight. Almonds soften best after 36 hours with one rinse ideally. This allows the water-soluble fats to be extracted via the blender.

· DO NOT USE THE SOAKING WATER IN YOUR MILK. While it may contain nutrients, it compromises the flavor of the finished product.

· Blend the batches in whatever size your blender can handle, but do not fill the blender more than two-thirds full. An overfull blender doesn't allow the water and soluble fats to emulsify.

· Use your blender's most powerful cycle and blend for as long as needed. If you don't wait long enough, you won't get a creamy milk.

Owen + Alchemy's Unsweetened Almond Milk

MAKES ½ GALLON

Pantry Essentials: **NUTS**

2½ quarts water

2 teaspoons Himalayan pink salt or sea salt

¾ pound raw almonds, soaked and drained

1 teaspoon good-quality vanilla extract or paste

Place all the ingredients in a high-speed blender and blend on high for 1 minute, or until the nuts and liquid have emulsified and the mixture is foamy. Depending on the power of your blender, this could take up to 5 minutes. Pour the mixture through a fine-mesh strainer or double layer of cheesecloth, and then strain it again. Transfer it to an airtight container and refrigerate it immediately. The milk will last for 5 days.

Spicy Tahini Avocado Toast

MAKES 2 SERVINGS (WITH SAUCE LEFT OVER)

Pantry Essential: **TAHINI**

I know what you're thinking: *Avocado toast? Really?!* Trendy, I know. But unlike a lot of food trends, I'm pretty confident this one is here to stay. I'm up for this combination any time of day. If you've never had avocado toast, you're in for a treat. I took it up a notch with this version, adding more creaminess and a little heat. The sprouts and shredded radishes are optional, but I love the crunch they give, and I'm always trying to add more plants wherever possible.

¼ cup tahini

¼ cup water

2 tablespoons fresh lemon juice

Red pepper flakes

Sea salt

1 avocado, roughly chopped

2 pieces gluten-free, sprouted, or bread of your choice, toasted

Sprouts and shredded radishes (optional)

In a small bowl, whisk together the tahini, water, lemon juice, and a pinch each of red pepper flakes and salt. Taste and add more salt or red pepper flakes if needed. In a separate bowl, mash the avocado with a fork until it is mostly smooth with a few lumps. Spread the mashed avocado on the two pieces of toast. Drizzle with tahini sauce. Top with sprouts and/or radishes.

KITCHEN NOTES: You'll have extra tahini sauce. Store it, covered, in the refrigerator and use it the next morning. You can freshen it up with a little splash of water or lemon juice.

Creamy Peach Porridge

MAKES 2-3 SERVINGS

Pantry Essentials: **COCONUT, SEEDS**

My son likes to eat the same thing for breakfast every day—some form of banana and almond butter. Sometimes it's straight-up, and other days it's whipped with some greens into a smoothie. It's A THING. As in, if we're out of bananas, my chill baby turns into a mini–King Kong, furiously stomping around our kitchen looking for his nanners. On one of these days, I whipped up this porridge to calm the beast. After a few bites, my mild-mannered little guy reemerged. Frozen peaches work great in this recipe, especially in the colder months when fresh ones aren't in season.

1 cup diced fresh (or thawed frozen) peaches

1 cup canned full-fat or light coconut milk

½ cup amaranth

1 teaspoon vanilla extract

1 teaspoon cinnamon

1–2 tablespoons real maple syrup
(depending on how sweet you like it)

Combine all the ingredients in a medium-size pot and bring the mixture to a boil. Reduce the heat, cover, and let it simmer for 20 minutes. Give it one stir during the 20 minutes to make sure it's not sticking to the bottom. If it is, reduce the heat a little. Remove the pot from the heat and keep it covered for 5 minutes before serving.

KITCHEN NOTES: You can store leftover porridge in the fridge for a couple of days. Do not be alarmed when you pull it out and it's one big hard slab of amaranth. This is normal, and it's because the coconut milk has hardened. Simply warm it on the stove over low heat, and it will return to its creamy texture again.

Blueberry Corn Cakes

MAKES 8 CAKES

Pantry Essentials: **NATURAL SWEETENER, GRAINS, COCONUT, GLUTEN-FREE FLOUR**

When I moved down South after living in Chicago for fifteen years, my sister asked if the move would influence the way I cooked. I'm not sure I've been here long enough to have fully realized my Southern belle potential in the kitchen, but I definitely wanted to include a recipe inspired by my new home of Charleston, South Carolina. Part cornbread, part pancake—these corn cakes are a riff on the South's classic hoecakes. Hoecakes are traditionally made with just cornmeal, boiling water, and salt. They're tasty, but feel like more of a snack than a full-on breakfast cake. So I added some coconut milk for richness and lots of maple syrup and berries.

1 cup canned full-fat coconut milk
(mix it well before measuring)

1 tablespoon apple cider vinegar

1 tablespoon flax meal

3 tablespoons water

1 cup coarse-ground cornmeal

½ cup brown rice flour

½ teaspoon baking soda

½ teaspoon sea salt

¼ cup real maple syrup, plus more for serving

1 teaspoon vanilla extract

1 cup blueberries, plus more for serving

2 tablespoons olive oil, plus more for cooking
the corn cakes

In a small bowl, combine the coconut milk and apple cider vinegar. In a separate small bowl, make a flax egg: mix the flax meal and water together. Set both the coconut milk mixture and the flax egg to the side and let them sit for at least 10 minutes.

In a large bowl, whisk together the cornmeal, rice flour, baking soda, and salt. Add maple syrup, vanilla, the coconut milk mixture, and the flax egg to the bowl. Stir together just until combined. Don't overstir. Add the blueberries and oil. Stir again.

Heat a little olive oil in a skillet over medium. When the oil is hot, scoop the batter onto the skillet, using about ¼ cup for each pancake. Watch for little bubbles to appear on top of each cake (this will take 3 to 5 minutes) and then flip it over. Cook until other side turns golden brown.

Serve with maple syrup and more berries.

Creamy Grits with Avocado and Hot Sauce

MAKES 4 SERVINGS

Pantry Essentials: **NUTS, VEGGIE BROTH, GRAINS, NUTRITIONAL YEAST**

My husband's dad, Tom, has made some of my favorite dishes of all time. His cheesy grits are probably #1. But over time, the "cheesy" part and my stomach weren't really getting along, so I decided to make a dairy-free version of his classic. One that is still as creamy and dreamy as the original, but with a new twist. These grits taste best right off the stove. They take about 20 minutes to make, so whip them up right before you're ready to serve.

3½ cups veggie broth, plus more if needed

½ cup raw cashews, soaked in water for at least a few hours (overnight is best), drained

1 tablespoon nutritional yeast

Cayenne

Sea salt

1 cup coarse-ground corn grits

Pepper

Toppings: diced avocado, hot sauce

Whiz ½ cup of the veggie broth with the cashews, nutritional yeast, a dash of cayenne, and a pinch of salt in high-speed blender until smooth. Depending on the speed of your blender, this might take up to 5 minutes.

Bring the remaining 3 cups veggie broth to a boil in a small pot. Add the grits and reduce heat. Stir continuously for 5 minutes. When there is a minute left, pour the cashew mixture into the pot and keep stirring. Add more veggie broth for desired consistency and add salt and pepper to your liking.

When you're ready to serve, top the grits with avocado, hot sauce, and more cayenne for an extra kick.

KITCHEN NOTES: If you use stone-ground grits for this recipe, you will need to increase the cooking time to 30 to 40 minutes, depending on the grain. If you have any leftovers, reheat them on the stove with some additional veggie broth to get the creamy texture back before serving.

Chilaquiles with Cilantro Cream

MAKES 4 SERVINGS

Pantry Essentials: **NUTS, BEANS**

Chilaquiles is one of those dishes where everyone has a strong opinion about the way it's supposed to be made. There are the red sauce lovers. There are the green sauce purists. I say anything goes, and I like every variety. This is the way we're currently eating them in my house—spicy, with lots of toppings and a creamy sauce. You can simmer the tortillas in the sauce or simply pour the sauce over some chips on a plate. Serve it however *you* like it!

FOR THE CILANTRO CREAM:

½ cup raw cashews, soaked in water for at least a few hours (overnight is best), drained

¼ cup cilantro

2 tablespoons fresh lime juice, or to taste

½ cup water, plus more if needed

Pinch of sea salt

FOR THE REST:

¾ cup veggie broth, plus more, if desired, for sautéing

Olive or coconut oil for sautéing, if desired

½ medium onion, diced (about 1 cup)

Dash of sea salt

1 (28-ounce) can crushed tomatoes

2 garlic cloves, chopped

1 chipotle pepper in adobo sauce

½ jalapeño, seeded and chopped

1 cup cooked pinto beans or black beans, drained and rinsed if canned

12 (8-inch) corn tortillas, cut into 8 pieces

Preheat the oven to 350 degrees.

To make the cilantro cream, place all the ingredients in a high-speed blender and blend until the mixture is completely smooth. This might take up to 5 minutes, depending on the power of your blender. Add more water as you go if needed. Taste and add more salt or lime juice if desired. Pour the cream into a small bowl and rinse your blender—you'll be using it again soon.

To finish the dish, heat a few tablespoons of veggie broth or a glug of oil in a large skillet over medium. When the pan is hot, add the onion and salt and sauté until the pieces are soft and translucent, about 5 minutes.

Combine the tomatoes, veggie broth, garlic, chipotle, and jalapeño in a blender and blend until the mixture is smooth. Pour it into the pan with the onion and bring it to a boil. Reduce the heat and simmer for 10 minutes.

While the sauce is simmering, spread the tortilla pieces on a baking sheet and bake for 5 to 15 minutes, until they begin to dry out and start to curl on the sides. If you aren't able to spread all the chips on your

TOPPING IDEAS:

Avocado

Hot sauce

Cilantro and onions

Diced peppers or tomatoes

KITCHEN NOTES: To save a little time, you can use store-bought tortilla chips instead of baking your own. You'll need about 6 cups.

sheet, do them in two batches or use two sheets. You can also spray the tortillas with a little olive oil for extra crispness.

Stir the beans into the sauce and simmer on low for a few more minutes. When you are ready to serve, stir the chips into the sauce—but only when you are ready to serve! You don't want them to get too soggy— you're aiming for a combination of soft and crunchy. Serve the chilaquiles warm, topped with cilantro cream and your chosen toppings.

Overnight Chia Oats

MAKES 2–3 SERVINGS

Pantry Essentials: **NATURAL SWEETENER, GRAINS, NUT MILK, COCONUT**

One of the greatest feelings in the morning is to look in the fridge and see your breakfast staring back at you all ready to go. No blending, chopping, or heating required—just a big jar of goodness that needs a spoon. This recipe makes a great base, but really comes together with some fun toppings. You can't go wrong, but if you are having a hard time deciding, I've listed my favorite combinations below.

FOR THE OATS:

1 cup rolled oats

1 cup canned full-fat coconut milk

½ cup almond milk, plus more if needed

1 teaspoon cinnamon

1 tablespoon chia seeds

Pinch of sea salt

Real maple syrup

CHOOSE A TOPPING COMBO:

Grapefruit, oranges, mint

Tahini and maple syrup

Roasted pineapple and coconut (page 183)

Almond butter and Strawberry Chia Jam (page 74)

Bananas and walnuts

Blueberries and basil

Combine all ingredients for the oats in a large jar with a lid. Stir in as much maple syrup you want to get the desired sweetness (start with a couple of teaspoons and go from there). Seal and refrigerate the mixture overnight. Taste it in the morning and add more almond milk if it's too gummy. Add toppings. Serve.

French Toast Sandwich with Cinnamon Cardamom Syrup

MAKES 4 SERVINGS

Pantry Essentials: **NUTS, PLANT-BASED MILK, COCONUT, NATURAL SWEETENER**

When I launched my website, one of the first media outlets to feature it was a morning show in Chicago called *You & Me This Morning*. I needed to make a plant-based breakfast that would look good on camera, was easy to prepare in the short segment time, and actually tasted good, too. No pressure! This was the dish I came up with. All went well, and I was invited back for another segment, so this recipe will always have a special place in my heart—along with the women who gave me a chance.

The Cinnamon Cardamom Syrup needs to be made a few days in advance to let the flavors meld. You can always use regular maple syrup here, but if you have the time, the spiced syrup really takes this dish to the next level.

FOR THE COCONUT CREAM:

1 (14-ounce) can full-fat coconut milk, refrigerated overnight

1 teaspoon real maple syrup

½ teaspoon vanilla extract

Dash of sea salt

FOR THE FRENCH TOAST:

½ cup raw cashews, soaked for a few hours (overnight is best), drained

1 cup unsweetened almond milk

½ cup water

1 teaspoon vanilla extract

1 teaspoon cinnamon

Dash of sea salt

Coconut oil

8 pieces gluten-free or sprouted bread, or your favorite bread

2 cups berries of your choice

Cinnamon Cardamom Syrup (recipe follows)

To make the coconut cream: Remove the coconut milk from the fridge—but don't shake the can. Open the can and remove the cream from the top (the cream and water will have separated), and transfer it to a medium-size bowl. You can discard the water or save it for smoothies. With a handheld mixer, blend the coconut cream with the maple syrup, vanilla, and salt until it reaches a whipped cream consistency. If you own an upright mixer, this will work great, too. If you don't have a mixer, do your best to whip with a fork or a whisk—it just won't be as creamy. Place it in the refrigerator until you're ready to use it.

To make the French toast: Combine the cashews, almond milk, water, vanilla, and salt in a high-speed blender and blend until the mixture is completely smooth. This might take up to 5 minutes, depending on the power of your blender. Pour the batter into a shallow bowl.

KITCHEN NOTES: If you don't have time to refrigerate the coconut milk overnight, there's no shame in buying premade coconut cream. A lot of grocery stores carry coconut whipped cream ready to go.

Place a medium-size skillet on the stovetop over medium heat and add a little coconut oil. Dip each side of the bread into the batter and then place it in the skillet. You want to make sure to just dip the bread in the batter on both sides—if you fully submerge it and let it sit, it will get soggy. Place dipped bread in the skillet (fit as many pieces as you can with enough room to flip) and cook on one side for 3 to 5 minutes (or until browned) and then flip it and cook the other side. Repeat with the remaining slices of bread.

Take a piece of the finished toast and spread the coconut cream on top. Add a layer of berries. Top with another piece of toast to make a sandwich. Add another dollop of cream and more berries. Add a little syrup on top and serve! This is definitely a knife-and-fork type of "sandwich."

Cinnamon Cardamom Syrup

MAKES ¾ CUP

Pantry Essential: **NATURAL SWEETENER**

¾ cup real maple syrup

1 cinnamon stick

½ teaspoon cardamom seeds or pods

Combine all the ingredients in a jar or bottle and seal. Every 24 hours, taste the syrup until you're happy with the flavor. The longer it sits, the more potent it will be. When it's ready, strain the syrup into a bowl and discard the cinnamon stick and pods. Return the syrup to the bottle. Use syrup on oatmeal, pancakes, or stirred into chia pudding. It will last for a few months stored in the fridge.

Breakfast Potato Bowl

MAKES 2-4 SERVINGS

Pantry Essential: **BEANS**

When I first changed my diet, going out to brunch with friends was pretty sad. It seemed like there was nothing on the menu that I could eat...with the exception of the big bowl of plain oatmeal. You know that bowl of oatmeal—the one buried at the bottom of every brunch menu? The oatmeal that makes you wonder, *Who would actually order that for brunch?* It was me. While my friends were devouring their cheesy omelets, I sat with a pouty frown, staring at a big bowl of blah. Guess what? No one wants a pouty baby at the brunch table—so I decided to get creative and join the party.

Enter the breakfast potato bowl. Nearly every brunch menu has some sort of home fries or hash brown situation happening. So I started ordering those and asking the kitchen to throw in the same veggies they would with one of their omelets—spinach, peppers, and onions. And it worked! Brunch became fun again, my friends didn't want to disown me, and I had a new recipe I could make at home on the weekends.

Olive or grape seed oil

2 medium-large potatoes, cut into 1-inch cubes (peeling is up to you)

1 orange or red bell pepper, seeded and diced

½ medium onion, diced

1 garlic clove, minced

Sea salt and pepper

Dash of paprika

1 cup cooked black beans, drained and rinsed, if canned

2 cups spinach, torn into small pieces

Toppings such as avocado, sprouts, hot sauce, salsa

Heat a generous glug of oil over medium in a large pan or cast-iron skillet. When the pan is hot, add the potatoes and cover. Cook for 10 minutes, until the potatoes begin to soften. Stir them every few minutes to make sure they aren't burning.

Add the bell pepper, onion, garlic, salt, pepper, and paprika. Cook for another 10 to 15 minutes, until the onions and peppers are soft and the potatoes are cooked through. Add the beans and spinach and cook for another few minutes, until the spinach begins to wilt and is nice and bright green. Serve the potatoes right away with avocado, sprouts, hot sauce, or your favorite toppings.

5 | Dips + Spreads + Sides

STRAWBERRY CHIA JAM AND CHOCOLATE CASHEW BUTTER

TAHINI HONEY SPREAD

VINSON PETRILLO'S FRESH CHICKPEA SPREAD WITH CRISPY BLACK OLIVES

ROASTED GARLIC BEAN DIP/SPREAD

CREAMY BABA GANOUSH

WHITE BEAN BUFFALO HUMMUS

JALAPEÑO CORN BREAD

BEET HORSERADISH RELISH/DIP/SPREAD

QUICK PICKLED DILL CUCUMBERS AND RADISHES

ZA'ATAR SWIRL BREAD

PERSIAN-STYLE DILL RICE

QUICK ROASTED SESAME BRUSSELS SPROUTS

FENNEL AND CABBAGE SLAW

HERB FRIES

ROASTED CARROTS WITH PESTO

LEBANESE SPICY POTATOES (BATATA HARRA)

CREAMY SUCCOTASH

MUSHROOM AND LENTIL STUFFING

Strawberry Chia Jam and Chocolate Cashew Butter

I like to have these two guys in the fridge at all times. The jam is great slathered on bread, spooned on top of oatmeal, and even drizzled over ice cream. I spread the cashew butter on some apple slices when I just NEED something sweet. Both are pretty low in sugar, which is not the case for most jams and chocolate spreads. Also, as I'm typing this, I just realized that these would actually taste pretty good together, too. Going to go try that out right now.

Strawberry Chia Jam

MAKES 1 CUP

Pantry Essential: **SEEDS**

2 cups fresh strawberries, hulled, or thawed frozen strawberries

1 teaspoon fresh lemon juice

2 teaspoons real maple syrup (to start, but you may need more, depending on how sweet the berries are)

2 tablespoons chia seeds

Place the berries, lemon juice, and maple syrup in a high-speed blender and blend until the mixture is well combined. Taste and add more maple syrup if needed. You can leave chunks of berries for a chunky jam or go super smooth.

Pour berry mixture into jar or container with a lid and stir in the chia seeds. Seal and refrigerate for a few hours or up to overnight to let the chia expand before serving. The jam will keep in the fridge for up to two weeks.

Chocolate Cashew Butter

MAKES 1 CUP

Pantry Essential: NUTS

1½ cups raw or roasted unsalted cashews

2 tablespoons cocoa powder

1–2 tablespoons real maple syrup or raw honey

3 tablespoons unsweetened almond milk, plus more if needed

In a food processor with the S blade attached, process the cashews to a smooth paste. This might take up to 10 minutes. Don't get discouraged—keep going. Eventually, it will become smooth. About every minute, make sure to scrape down the sides of the food processor to incorporate any rogue cashew bits.

When the mixture is smooth, add the cocoa powder, maple syrup or honey, and almond milk. Add more almond milk if needed to reach the desired consistency. Store the cashew butter in the fridge in an airtight container for a few weeks.

Tahini Honey Spread

MAKES ¾ CUP

Pantry Essentials: **TAHINI, NATURAL SWEETENER**

This is a great multipurpose spread or drizzle for everything from toast and oatmeal to ice cream and biscuits. I love changing it up every time by adding a different mix-in—rosewater is my favorite. Because tahini and honey are both pretty strong flavors, take it easy with your mix-in, adding a little bit at a time and tasting as you go (especially with the rosewater).

¾ cup tahini

2–3 tablespoons raw honey

Sea salt

Mix-in ideas: rosewater, cinnamon, cayenne

Combine the tahini, 2 tablespoons of honey, and a pinch of salt. Taste and add more honey or salt if needed. Stir in your chosen flavoring to the whole batch or for each serving. Store the spread refrigerated in an airtight container for up to two weeks.

Vinson Petrillo's Fresh Chickpea Spread with Crispy Black Olives

MAKES 6 SERVINGS

Pantry Essential: **BEANS**

After we shot this recipe for the cookbook, the leftovers disappeared quickly. Every time one of us walked by this spread, we dipped whatever we could in it—leftover veggies, scraps of bread, a straight-up spoon! It's just so fresh and delicious. Which was no surprise, because it's Vinson Petrillo's recipe.

Vinson is the executive chef at Zero Café + Bar, which is in the prettiest hotel I've ever seen, Zero George in Charleston. Vinson has won a big television cooking show and appeared on another, but when I met him in his kitchen for the first time, he was a pretty low-key dude. He was focused on one thing: the food. This recipe is so versatile—if you can't find fresh chickpeas, Vinson suggests using thawed frozen peas or fava beans and notes that you can also swap in any fresh herbs you have on hand in place of the dill.

1 pound fresh chickpeas (garbanzo beans), peeled

4 ounces baby spinach (about 4 cups)

1 garlic clove, chopped fine

Juice of 2 lemons

16 mint leaves

1 cup good-quality olive oil, plus more for serving

Sea salt and pepper

2 cups domestic black olives, pits removed

Grilled bread for serving

Handful fresh dill

Bring a pot of heavily salted water to a boil and set a bowl of ice water nearby. Working in batches, blanch the chickpeas in the boiling water just until they are tender and bright green. Remove them from the pot and quickly shock them in the ice bath. Place the chickpeas in a food processor with the spinach, garlic, lemon juice, and mint. Turn the processor on high and begin slowly pouring the olive oil in a thin stream into the chickpea mixture so that it will emulsify. Once the mixture comes together, taste and season it with salt and pepper. Place it in an airtight container until you're ready to serve.

If the olives are in brine, strain them to remove any moisture. Cut them in half and arrange them evenly on two dehydrator trays. Set the temperature to 160 degrees and leave them for 8 to 12 hours until they become hard. (If you do not own a dehydrator,

KITCHEN NOTES: If you don't have time to dehydrate the olives, just dice them finely and press them with a clean kitchen towel to remove as much moisture as possible.

arrange the olives on a cooling rack set on a sheet tray and put them in the oven at lowest possible temperature for 4 hours until crisp.) Once the olives have hardened, put them in the food processor and pulse until they resemble soil.

Serve the chickpea spread on grilled bread; carefully spoon some of the crispy olive soil on top. Garnish with fresh dill and a few drops of good-quality olive oil.

Roasted Garlic Bean Dip/Spread

MAKES 4 SERVINGS

Pantry Essential: BEANS

I love garlic. A lot. But there is something about raw garlic that doesn't always jive with my tummy. I roasted the garlic for this spread, and it really seems to help on the digestion front. It does take a little bit of time, but the richness and flavor it adds to this dip, along with the roasted garlic aroma that fills your kitchen, make it worth the effort. Serve it as a dip with veggies, spread it on a sandwich in place of mayo, or mix a little into a salad.

1 head of garlic

1 teaspoon plus 2 tablespoons good olive oil

1 (15-ounce) can cannellini beans, drained and rinsed, or 1¾ cups cooked beans

3 tablespoons fresh lemon juice, or to taste

¼ cup Italian parsley

Sea salt

Preheat the oven to 400 degrees. Chop off the very top of the garlic (the pointed end) to expose the cloves. Use 1 teaspoon of the oil to drizzle over the exposed top. Place the garlic on a piece of aluminum foil and bring up the sides to make a little sealed tent. Roast it for 35 to 45 minutes. You'll know it's finished when the cloves are soft and golden brown. Let the garlic cool and carefully push out the cloves. It's OK if they get a little smashed; they are going to be all blended up anyway.

Combine the garlic with the remaining 2 tablespoons of oil, the lemon juice, parsley, and a pinch of salt in a food processor and process until the mixture is smooth. You'll still see lots of parsley chunks, and that's OK. Taste and add more salt or lemon juice if needed. Serve the spread immediately or store it refrigerated in an airtight container for up to a week.

Creamy Baba Ganoush

MAKES 4-6 SERVINGS

Pantry Essential: **TAHINI**

Yes, all baba ganoush could be considered creamy. But I swear this one is creamier than most. I whipped in a little sautéed onion and garlic to up its richness and creaminess status. The recipe calls for charring the eggplant on your stovetop. If you've got a grill, that works even better. Don't be scared if you've never charred veggies before. You're going to feel really proud when you pull it off (I still do).

2 medium eggplants

Coconut or olive oil

1 cup chopped onions

2 garlic cloves, diced

¼ cup tahini

Juice of 1 small lemon, or to taste

Red pepper flakes (optional)

Sea salt

KITCHEN NOTES: If you don't have a gas burner or a grill, broil the eggplant until it chars. Just make sure to watch it closely!

TASTERS TELL ALL...

"I will admit, I was intimidated by this recipe—but the end product was incredible. We had people over the night I made it, and it was the most popular thing on the table. Everyone was shocked it was homemade!"

Preheat the oven to 375 degrees. Line a baking sheet with parchment paper.

Poke the eggplants a few times with a fork around all sides. Using tongs (or very brave hands), place the eggplant on your burner over a gas flame for a few minutes on each side. The longer you char the sides, the smokier the baba ganoush will be.

Place the charred eggplants on the prepared baking sheet and roast them for 15 to 20 minutes or until they get completely soft and start to collapse.

Meanwhile, heat a glug of oil in a medium pan on medium high heat. When the oil is hot, sauté the onions and garlic until they begin to caramelize and brown.

Let the eggplants cool enough to handle, then peel away the skin, remove the stems, and scrape the "guts" into a high-speed blender or food processor. Add the onions, garlic, tahini, and lemon juice. If you want to add a little heat, throw in a pinch of red pepper flakes.

Pulse until you reach your desired consistency—make the baba ganoush super smooth or keep it a little chunky. Add a little more lemon juice if needed. Salt to taste. Store the baba ganoush sealed in the refrigerator for a few days.

White Bean Buffalo Hummus

MAKES 4–6 SERVINGS

Pantry Essentials: **TAHINI, NATURAL SWEETENER**

Hummus without chickpeas? Oh, yes. I don't have anything against chickpeas, but when it comes to hummus, sometimes I like to mix it up and use other beans or legumes. Some people have a really difficult time digesting chickpeas. If you've ever noticed that you're super gassy after eating a tub of hummus, you might be one of them. Northern and cannellini beans make a great substitute.

My favorite way to eat this hummus is to spread it on a charred tortilla and then load it up with veggies and herbs.

1 (15-ounce) can northern or cannellini beans, drained and rinsed, or 1¾ cups cooked beans

¼ cup tahini

2–3 tablespoons buffalo sauce (see Kitchen Notes)

½ teaspoon real maple syrup

2–3 tablespoons fresh lemon juice

Sea salt

In a food processor with the S blade attached, pulse the beans, tahini, 2 tablespoons of buffalo sauce, maple syrup, 2 tablespoons of lemon juice, and a pinch of salt to a smooth paste. Add more salt and lemon juice if needed and more buffalo sauce to get the spice level you love. Store the hummus covered in the fridge for up to a week.

KITCHEN NOTES: When shopping for buffalo sauce, make sure to read labels carefully. Look for brands that don't contain extra sugars or dairy products. Tessemae's is my favorite.

Jalapeño Corn Bread

MAKES 6-8 SERVINGS

Pantry Essentials: PLANT-BASED MILK, GRAINS, SEEDS, NATURAL SWEETENER, GLUTEN-FREE FLOUR

Corn bread has always been a good friend of mine, and because of that, I've never been too picky about how it's served. Whether it's a big hunk topped with honey, in a bowl with some hearty chili, or eaten with collard greens... I'm pretty excited by it every time. Except when it's dry. I've had my heart broken more than once when I've bought a piece of delicious-looking cornbread and brought it home, only to watch it turn to crumbles as I unwrap it. I've tried hard to make sure your heart doesn't get broken here. This bread is soft and bouncy and chewy. It's not super sweet, so feel free to drizzle on some honey or maple syrup at the end to make it sweeter.

1 cup unsweetened almond milk

1 tablespoon apple cider vinegar

1 tablespoon flax meal

3 tablespoons water

1 cup cornmeal (I like medium-grind)

½ cup almond meal

½ cup brown rice flour

2 teaspoons aluminum-free baking powder

1 teaspoon sea salt

¼ cup real maple syrup

2 jalapeños, seeded and sliced

3 tablespoons olive oil

Raw honey or real maple syrup

INSIDER TIP!

I asked the cornmeal king, Glenn Roberts of Anson Mills, how to buy the best cornmeal. Here's what he said: "Source 100 percent coarse cornmeal that is fresh milled at your local small grain mill when possible. Always store it frozen to retain the bright flavors and nutrition."

Preheat the oven to 400 degrees. Grease an 8-inch square pan or line it with parchment paper.

In a small bowl, combine the almond milk and apple cider vinegar. In another small bowl, make a flax egg: mix the flax meal and water together. Set both the almond milk mixture and the flax egg aside and let them sit for at least 10 minutes.

In a large bowl, mix the cornmeal, almond meal, rice flour, baking powder, and salt together. Add the almond milk mixture, flax egg, maple syrup, and half of the jalapeño slices. Stir to combine, but do not overstir. Add the olive oil and give it a few more stirs.

Pour the batter into your prepared pan. Spread the remaining jalapeños on top. Bake for 20 minutes or until a fork or toothpick inserted in the center comes out clean. Let it cool for 10 to 15 minutes before serving.

KITCHEN NOTES: If you don't get around to eating this all before it gets a little stale, dice the remaining bread into cubes and toast them in the oven to make cornbread croutons.

Beet Horseradish Relish/Dip/Spread

MAKES 8-10 SERVINGS

Pantry Essential: **NATURAL SWEETENER**

On a recent visit with my Dad and Deb (my stepmom), I was poking around their fridge looking for a snack and came across a tub of pretty pink stuff. I say "stuff" because I wasn't quite sure if it was a relish, a dip, or a spread. That didn't stop me, and I jumped in with a spoon. It turned out to be beets and horseradish, one of my favorite flavor combinations. Traditionally this combo is made to accompany meat and fish, but that night I tossed it around with some salty boiled potatoes and then also used it as a dressing for a giant salad. Make yourself a batch and decide for yourself—is this is a relish, dip, or spread (or all three)?

2 medium beets, washed (you can use precooked, if you prefer)

Sea salt

3 tablespoons prepared horseradish

1 tablespoon real maple syrup, or to taste

2 teaspoons apple cider vinegar, or to taste

To cook the beets, chop off the greens, leaving about an inch on top; discard the greens or save them for another use. Boil the beets in a pot of water with a pinch of salt until they are soft enough to pierce through with a knife, about 40 minutes. Let them cool, then slide off and toss away the skin.

Grate the cooked beets and combine all the ingredients. Taste and add more vinegar, salt, or maple syrup if needed.

KITCHEN NOTES: When buying jarred horseradish, make sure to read the label. A lot of brands contain sugar and unnecessary additives. Gold's makes a great prepared horseradish. You can also use fresh horseradish. If you decide to grate your own, you may need to up the vinegar and salt a little in this recipe.

Quick Pickled Dill Cucumbers and Radishes

MAKES 4–10 SERVINGS

Pantry Essential: **NATURAL SWEETENER**

I think it's super cool when someone pickles vegetables the old-fashioned way or ferments their own sauerkraut... just sitting back and waiting patiently while the process works its magic. Unfortunately, I'm not that patient. If you're anything like me, this quick pickle recipe will soon become a favorite. It doesn't take long for the magic to happen here. These little pickles are great on sandwiches, thrown into a salad, or eaten standing in front of the fridge.

1 cup apple cider vinegar

1 cup water

1 teaspoon sea salt

1 tablespoon raw honey or real maple syrup

2 garlic cloves, crushed

8 medium-large radishes, thinly sliced

1 cucumber, thinly sliced

½ cup minced fresh dill

In a small pot, bring the vinegar, water, salt, and honey to a boil. Let the liquid cool.

Drop a piece of garlic into the bottom of a 24-ounce jar with a lid. Alternate layers of cucumbers and radishes in the jar, sprinkling a little dill on each layer. Drop the other piece of garlic on the top. Pour the vinegar mixture over the veggies. Put the lid on tight and rock the jar back and forth a few times. Store it in the fridge for a few hours before you dig in. These will taste best the next day (if you can wait that long), and they'll last for about a week.

KITCHEN NOTES: If you have a mandoline, it will work great here. If not, just cut the veggies as thin as you can!

Notes from the Field:
Sisterhood of the Traveling Plants

———

Eating OPP in your home is one thing; fitting in plant-based meals on the road is another. But just like you map out the route for your road trip, dig through drawers to find your passport, or make sure you pack enough clean underwear, you can also plan ahead with your food.

Never in a thousand years would I have imagined that one day I'd actually seek out plant-based foods when traveling. Vacation and work travel used to mean that all bets were off and I could eat whatever I wanted. But at the same time, I used to end up with pretty bad bellyaches on most of those trips, and eventually, the splurge just didn't seem worth it.

Now I make it a priority to plan ahead—eating plant-based on the road actually makes travel more enjoyable for me. On vacations, I have more energy to explore, and my reentry into life at home is way easier when I don't feel sick. On work trips, I'm more efficient and don't feel as tired in long meetings.

It's not about being perfect. If there's some weird roadside food truck that's calling your name or a restaurant you've read about and have been dying to try, DO IT. But also do your best to get in one plant-based meal a day in addition your other food adventures. Whether you're traveling for work or for fun, here are some tips that can help keep you OPP on the road.

Find at least one plant-based friendly restaurant before you leave.

Before I travel, I search my destination online with the keywords *vegetarian* or *vegan* and *restaurant*. I usually get at least one good hit from a magazine/newspaper or local blogger of where to go. The restaurant doesn't have to be a full-on veg place; just scan the menu and make sure there's at least one thing you can eat. I make sure to email myself the list of names, so when I get there, I know exactly where I'm headed.

I especially love the site and app Happy Cow. It finds all the plant-based-friendly restaurants in your vicinity. It even lists the local health food stores.

Have some emergency snacks ready to go.

You never know when you're going to get stuck in an airport and the only thing open is a frozen yogurt stand. Or when you'll be in the car with fifty miles to go before you'll have another option for lunch besides the Micky D's. Whether you're driving or flying, it's always a good idea to have a stash of snacks on hand. I usually have a packet or two of Justin's Almond Butter and an apple, a nice mix of nuts and seeds, and a hummus pack. If you're a super planner, make some granola (page 54), some pistachio squares (page 212), or an easy salad that won't get soggy for the plane. Ball jars work great for travel.

Shop when you get there or ship what you need.

My sister Alissa travels a lot for her job and doesn't have time to shop before each trip, so she shops when she gets to her destination. She finds the closest grocery store to her hotel and buys snacks and ingredients to make quickie meals in her room.

If she knows she'll be busy from the moment she hits the ground, she'll also ship things to her hotel in advance. It's an awesome idea if your budget allows. There are a lot of healthy brands that ship juices, snacks, and ready-to-go meals. It's so nice to start each day knowing you'll fit in your plants no matter how long your meeting lasts.

Do your best.

When you're on the road, sometimes your only option may be a place that might not have the most ideal offerings. But you have to eat, so do your best. I was stuck in an airport once, and the only option was pizza. So I ordered a slice with no cheese and then had them double the sauce and load up the veggies—as in every vegetable they had. Was it my most nourishing lunch ever? No. But I wasn't going to starve myself because I couldn't find the perfect meal. And I was a much nicer person with food in my belly when I landed.

When I'm traveling, I often look to Indian, Mexican, Thai, and Mediterranean restaurants. I know I can always find options there. The good news is that more and more restaurants are jumping on the plant-based wagon, so it's becoming easier than ever to find plant-based meals just about anywhere you go.

Za'atar Swirl Bread

MAKES 8 SERVINGS

Pantry Essentials: **SEEDS, GLUTEN-FREE FLOUR**

One of the biggest fears I had about writing a cookbook was screwing up a classic recipe by putting my spin on it. The traditional Middle Eastern spice blend za'atar is one of those recipes. I've seen it made so many ways that it's hard to know the "right" one. Some blends have oregano, and some don't. Sometimes the spices are ground with a mortar and pestle, and sometimes they're kept whole. I fretted over this (way too long) before I decided to just go with my favorite ingredients and not worry about the za'atar police judging my style. Feel free to play around with this recipe to suit your own taste.

Za'atar bread is a popular way of using this spice, and it usually consists of spreading the blend on pita and baking it. I wanted to make a gluten-free and prettier version by swirling the spice in instead. Channel your inner artist and get creative with making your swirl (or just use the instructions I've offered below). I'll tell you straight up, this bread doesn't have a traditionally bready texture—it's a little spongier and denser than bread made with white flour. But I love it.

2 tablespoons ground sumac (see sidebar)

5 teaspoons sesame seeds, toasted

1 tablespoon dried thyme

½ teaspoon sea salt

3 tablespoons olive oil, plus more for the pan

1 cup chickpea (garbanzo bean) flour

1 cup warm water

First, make the za'atar mixture: In a small bowl, combine the sumac, sesame seeds, thyme, salt, and oil. Set the mixture aside to let the flavors meld until your batter is ready.

Add the flour to a medium bowl and stir in a little water at a time until you have a thin batter. Set it aside for 2 hours.

Preheat the oven to 350 and grease an 8-or 9-inch round pan (I like using a cast-iron skillet for this). Pour the batter into the pan. Drop and scatter ½-teaspoon-size scoops of your za'atar spice mixture on top of the batter. It should look like za'atar polka dots. With a knife or skewer, zigzag and swirl through the batter from one side of the pan to the other. Make sure you go all the way to the edges; you want to be sure to distribute the spices throughout.

Bake the bread for 25 to 30 minutes, until the edges begin to brown and the dough pulls slightly away from the sides. Let it cool for at least 5 minutes. Cut and serve. This bread makes a great appetizer to go with dips and spreads, especially hummus and baba ganoush.

What Is Sumac?

———

Sumac is one of the main ingredients in za'atar. If you've never tried or bought it, I'm really excited for you to add it to your spice rotation. It is produced from sumac berries and has a deep, bright, rich red color (even prettier than paprika). It has a tangy lemon flavor that makes it perfect to sprinkle on veggies and on top of dips and spreads. While sumac is gaining popularity in the States, it can still be tricky to find in stores. I usually purchase mine online, because the prices seem to be a little better for the quantity I like to buy (which is a lot).

Persian-Style Dill Rice

MAKES 4-6 SERVINGS

Pantry Essentials: **GRAINS, VEGGIE BROTH**

Please note the *style* I added after *Persian* in the recipe title—this is a riff on a very classic dish. Traditionally, Persian dill rice has a *tahdig*—a crispy browned layer of rice that is achieved by frying it in the bottom the pan with oil and saffron, and sometimes yogurt. It's ridiculously delicious, but most weeknights it's not in the cards to pull off. This is my quickie version. If you do have the time and want to learn more about it, there are a lot of great demos online that can show you how to make the perfect *tahdig*. It's a pretty cool process, and I highly recommend trying it out.

1 cup basmati white rice, rinsed under cool water

1 cup veggie broth

¾ cup water

1 teaspoon olive oil

Sea salt

1 cup fresh or thawed frozen lima beans

½–1 cup chopped fresh dill

¼ cup fresh lemon juice, or more if needed

Combine the rice, broth, water, oil, and a big pinch of salt in a medium saucepan. Let the mixture soak for 20 minutes. Bring the rice to a boil and then reduce the heat to maintain a simmer. Add the lima beans and cover. Simmer for 12 to 15 minutes, until the rice is cooked through and no water remains. Remove it from the heat and keep it covered for 5 minutes.

Stir in the dill and lemon juice. I like A LOT of dill, so I use the full cup. If you're not sure, start with ½ cup and see what you think. Add salt to taste and more lemon juice if needed.

Quick Roasted Sesame Brussels Sprouts

MAKES 4 SERVINGS

Pantry Essential: **SEEDS**

Over the last five years, it seems like Brussels sprouts have gone from being one of the most hated vegetables of all time to one of the most popular. They began popping up on the best restaurant menus, and then those same restaurants started taking them off the menu because they feared they were too trendy. It's hard to keep up, so I don't and just eat what I love. Cool or not cool, Brussels are here to stay with me, and this is my favorite way to prepare them: a little charring on the stovetop and then softening them up in the oven. If you've got a cast-iron skillet, pull it out for this recipe.

1½ tablespoons olive or grape seed oil

1 pound Brussels sprouts, cut in half

2 tablespoons red wine vinegar, or more if needed

1 tablespoon tamari or coconut aminos

2 teaspoons sesame seeds (I prefer toasted)

Pinch of red pepper flakes

Sea salt

Preheat the oven to 375 degrees. On the stovetop, heat a cast-iron skillet or oven-safe skillet over medium and add the oil. When it's hot, add the Brussels sprouts, cut sides down. Cook for 8 minutes or until they start to brown on the bottom.

Remove the pan from the stovetop. Add 1 tablespoon of vinegar and give the sprouts a stir. Place them in the oven for about 15 minutes or until they are nice and tender. Remove and immediately add the other tablespoon of vinegar, along with the tamari, sesame seeds, and red pepper flakes. Toss until the sprouts are nice and coated with seeds and flakes. Add salt to taste and more vinegar if needed. Serve.

Fennel and Cabbage Slaw

MAKES 6 SERVINGS

Pantry Essential: **NATURAL SWEETENER**

Whether you're a part-time or full-time plant-based eater, planning ahead is crucial—especially when it comes to social situations like parties and barbecues. Unless your host is down with OPP, there may be few options for you. I always try to plan ahead by asking the host if I can bring a dish to share, and this slaw is one of my go-tos.

4 cups shredded green cabbage
(about ½ medium cabbage)

2 carrots, shredded

2 green onions, thinly sliced
(use white part of the onion, not the green top)

1 fennel bulb, fronds removed, thinly sliced

½ cup apple cider vinegar, or to taste

2 tablespoons raw honey, or to taste

2 tablespoons olive oil

Sea salt and pepper

In a large bowl, combine the cabbage, carrots, green onions, and fennel. In a small bowl, whisk together the vinegar and honey. Add the oil and whisk again. Pour the dressing onto the cabbage and use your hands to toss the veggies to make sure everything gets coated. Salt and pepper to taste. Add more vinegar or honey if needed. If you have leftovers, store them refrigerated in an airtight container for up to 2 weeks.

Herb Fries

MAKES 3-4 SERVINGS

Pantry Essential: **NUTRITIONAL YEAST**

Fries are definitely a gateway food that can help your family transition into a plant-based diet. Tossing the fries with nutritional yeast and fresh herbs ups the traditional baked fry game and gives them a zesty flavor. I used parsley and rosemary here, but feel free to use any fresh herbs you have on hand.

These fries are great served alongside a big fat veggie burger (Hilary's are my favorite brand) loaded with your favorite toppings, or smothered in the White Bean Pepper Chili (page 165).

3 medium Yukon gold potatoes (up to you if you want to peel them)

Olive or grape seed oil

1 tablespoon nutritional yeast

Sea salt and pepper

1 tablespoon minced Italian parsley

1 teaspoon minced fresh rosemary

KITCHEN NOTES: If you want to sub in sweet potatoes for the Yukons, skip the parboiling step and go straight to tossing them with the oil and seasoning. Bake for 15 minutes, flip them, and then continue baking for another 10 to 15 minutes, or until they're crisp. Finish them the same way, with herbs and a little more salt.

Preheat the oven to 450 degrees and line a rimmed baking sheet with parchment paper.

Cut the potatoes into sticks ¼-to ½-inch square on the ends.

In a large pot, bring 3 to 4 inches of water to a boil. Remove the pot from the heat, put the potatoes in the water, and cover them for 10 minutes. Make sure to set a timer—you don't want them to sit any longer than that. Drain the potatoes.

About 5 minutes before you plan to bake the fries, put the baking sheet in the oven to heat.

While the pan is heating, toss the potatoes in a bowl with a glug of oil, nutritional yeast, and some salt and pepper. Spread the potatoes on the hot pan, and put them in the oven. Every 5 minutes or so, toss the fries around with a spatula to make sure they are cooking evenly. Bake until they are golden brown (25 to 35 minutes, depending on how crispy you want them).

Sprinkle on the herbs and a little more salt. Serve hot.

Roasted Carrots with Pesto

MAKES 4 SERVINGS

Pantry Essential: **NUTS**

Growing up, I used to think that carrots with the big leafy green tops were just something that existed in cartoons. The bags of carrots my mom brought home didn't have them, and I never saw them at the grocery store. It wasn't until I got older that I realized that those cartoon carrots were real! You'll definitely have the easiest time finding them at a farmers' market, but a lot of grocery stores carry them, too. The best part about these carrots is that they're sort of the BOGO (buy one, get one free) of vegetables—you'll get two ingredients out of one veggie. Try to buy organic carrots if you're going to make the pesto portion of this recipe.

2 bunches of organic carrots with leafy green tops (10 to 12 carrots)

Olive, grape seed, or coconut oil

Sea salt and pepper

2 garlic cloves, peels left on

⅓ cup walnuts

1 tightly packed cup basil

Nutritional yeast (optional)

¼–½ cup good olive oil

2–4 tablespoons fresh lemon juice

Preheat the oven to 400 degrees and line a large rimmed baking sheet with parchment paper. You want to make sure the carrots have some space as they roast, so use two baking sheets if necessary. Trim the greens from the carrots, leaving about 2 inches at the top. Set aside 1 cup, loosely packed, of the leafiest parts of the greens (no stems); discard or save any extra for another use. If the carrots are really large, cut them lengthwise.

Toss the carrots in a little oil, with salt and pepper to taste. Roast them for 30 to 40 minutes, until tender.

While the carrots are in the oven, do a "quick roast" of the garlic on the stovetop. Put the cloves in a small pan over medium-high and cover. Toss the garlic around every 30 seconds or so until it forms black/dark brown spots and softens. This should take about 5 minutes. Let them cool and remove the skins. You can use the same pan to toast the walnuts. Keep the pan on medium-high heat and toast the walnuts for about 5 minutes. Make sure to stir continuously, as you want to make sure they toast and not burn.

In a food processor with the S blade attached, blend the walnuts, garlic, carrot tops, basil, and a pinch of nutritional yeast, if you're using it. While the motor is still running, drizzle in about 1/4 cup of the olive oil and 2 tablespoons of the lemon juice. Taste and add salt or more lemon juice, oil, or nutritional yeast if needed.

Spoon the pesto over the carrots before serving.

Lebanese Spicy Potatoes (Batata Harra)

MAKES 3-4 SERVINGS

Pantry Essential: **TAHINI**

Traditionally, the potatoes in this dish are deep-fried. I'm not opposed to frying things; I'm just opposed to the mess I make trying to fry things. I also really like that this version is a little lighter on the belly. Fried or not, I think the true hero of this dish is the garlic. There's a lot of it. But then the lemon juice, red pepper, and cilantro bring it all together like one big happy family. If you're not a cilantro fan, you can easily sub in some fresh parsley.

2 large Yukon gold potatoes or 8 baby reds, cut into 1-inch cubes

Sea salt

Olive, coconut, or grape seed oil

6 garlic cloves, minced

1 teaspoon red pepper flakes

1–2 tablespoons fresh lemon juice

⅓ cup chopped cilantro

¼ cup tahini

Fill a medium pot with water and add the potato cubes and a pinch of salt. Bring the water to a boil, then reduce the heat to simmer until the potatoes are fork-tender, 10 to 15 minutes. Drain.

In a medium pan, heat a little oil on medium heat and add garlic. Move the garlic around in the pan for 30 seconds or so, until it becomes fragrant. Add the red pepper flakes and stir for another minute. Add the potatoes and toss them in the pan to get them coated as much as possible with the garlic and red pepper. Cook for a couple minutes, moving them around the pan. Add the lemon juice, toss around again to coat. Stir in the cilantro. Add a couple pinches of salt and toss one more time before serving with a drizzle of tahini.

Creamy Succotash

Pantry Essentials: **COCONUT, BEANS**

Until I started researching for this book, I had no idea that 99 percent of succotash recipes call for tomatoes and peppers. What kind of succotash world had I been living in? What else had my parents not told me? Regardless, I forgive them, because I actually prefer my family's tomato-and-pepper-free recipe.

The only thing I changed from their version was to replace all of the butter (we're talking multiple sticks here) with coconut milk to achieve the rich, creamy dish I grew up loving.

1½ cups canned light coconut milk

1½ cups lima beans (a.k.a. butter beans)

Kernels from 4 ears of cooked corn (see Kitchen Notes)

Pinch of cayenne

Sea salt and pepper

Combine the coconut milk, beans, corn, and cayenne in a small pot and bring it to a boil. Reduce the heat and simmer on low for 40 minutes to an hour, or until most of the coconut milk is absorbed. Make sure to watch the pot and stir a few times while it cooks. Add salt and pepper to taste.

KITCHEN NOTES: After you've cut the corn off the cob, make sure to take the back of your knife and run it along the cob to get out all the juice and corn "milk" that remains. This will make the dish even creamier.

Mushroom and Lentil Stuffing

MAKES 6-8 SERVINGS

Pantry Essential: LENTILS

If I were going to power rank the all-time greatest side dishes, stuffing would make my Top Five. When I changed my diet, I thought it might not be something I'd ever be able to have again because of all the butter and bread that's in most stuffing recipes. I quickly decided that this couldn't happen and went to the kitchen to create a version I could eat. This is it.

Olive oil

1 cup dry black lentils

2½–4 cups veggie broth

1 teaspoon dried sage

1 teaspoon dried thyme

1 teaspoon cumin

16 ounces bella or white mushrooms (or a combination), sliced

2 garlic cloves, minced

1 tablespoon tamari or coconut aminos

1 large onion, chopped

4 celery stalks, chopped

2 tablespoons chopped fresh sage

½ teaspoon minced fresh thyme

Sea salt

Pinch of cayenne

11 cups (about 1 loaf) sprouted, gluten-free, or sourdough bread torn into 1-inch chunks and left on a baking sheet overnight

Pepper

Grease a large baking dish or cast-iron pan with olive oil.

Rinse the lentils under water and pick out any duds. In a small pot, combine the lentils with enough of the broth to cover them, plus about 1 inch (you'll need about 1½ cups), and stir in the dried herbs and cumin. Bring the broth to a boil and reduce the heat to simmer until the lentils are soft, but still a little firm. This will take 25 to 30 minutes. Make sure to watch the pot and add more of the broth or some water if needed to cover the lentils. Taste them as you go to make sure they don't overcook and get mushy. Drain any excess liquid that isn't absorbed.

When the lentils are almost finished, preheat the oven to 350 degrees.

In a large pan, heat a glug of olive oil or a few tablespoons of the veggie broth over medium. When the pan is hot, add the mushrooms, garlic, and tamari. Cook the mixture until the mushrooms are soft and release their liquid. Add the cooked lentils, onion, celery, fresh herbs, and a generous pinch of salt. Cook until the veggies are soft, about 10 minutes. Add 1 cup of the veggie broth and stir in the cayenne, 3 tablespoons olive oil, and some cracked pepper.

Place the bread chunks in a large bowl and pour the mushroom and lentil mixture over them. (If you don't have a bowl large enough, you can do this in batches.) Toss until everything is combined. Add ¼ to ½ cup more broth if the bread needs more moisture. It shouldn't be soggy, but shouldn't be dry either.

Transfer the stuffing to the prepared baking dish or cast-iron skillet. Cover it with foil and bake for 40 minutes or until the bread is cooked through. Remove the foil and bake until the top of the stuffing is browned and crispy, about 15 minutes.

6 | Soups + Salads

TOMATO AND WHITE BEAN PANZANELLA

KALE AVOCADO SALAD

CARROT AND PISTACHIO SALAD

JERUSALEM SALAD

DANIEL HOLZMAN'S CHOPPED VEGETABLE SALAD

QUINOA TACO SALAD

TOMATO AND CORN SALAD WITH JALAPEÑO-LIME DRESSING

CREAMY MILLET SALAD

POMEGRANATE, SPINACH, AND WALNUT SALAD

RED LENTIL SOUP

EASY SPICY MISO SOUP

ROASTED CAULIFLOWER AND FENNEL SOUP

ROASTED POTATO, CORN, AND LEEK CHOWDER

THAI COCONUT SOUP

CREAMY ROASTED TOMATO SOUP

RUTH REICHL'S BUTTERNUT SQUASH SOUP

Tomato and White Bean Panzanella

MAKES 6 SERVINGS

Pantry Essential: **BEANS**

When I left Chicago, my good friends Sam and Anne threw a little going-away party for me. That night, Sam made the best panzanella I've ever had. I asked him if could riff on his recipe for the book, and he said yes, but under one condition—I couldn't call it "Samzanella." Hmmm. I switched up his version a little by reducing the oil, adding some white beans, and then sprinkling on some red pepper flakes to give it a tiny bit of spice—I call it the Samzanella Remix. Sorry, buddy. If you're going to give me a good food pun...I'm going to have to use it.

5 cups crusty bread, cut or torn into 1-inch cubes (see Kitchen Notes)

¼ cup olive oil, plus more for toasting

Sea salt

Pinch of red pepper flakes

4 cups chopped tomatoes (I like to use a combination of different tomatoes, including some quartered cherry tomatoes)

1 small red onion, shaved or sliced very thin

1 cup cooked cannellini beans, drained and rinsed if canned

2 garlic cloves, smashed with the flat of a knife

12 large basil leaves, torn

3 tablespoons red wine vinegar

Preheat the oven to 350 degrees and get a baking sheet ready.

Toss the bread with a glug of oil, a pinch of salt, and the red pepper flakes. Toast it in the oven for 8 to 10 minutes, until the bread is slightly crunchy on the outside and still a little soft in the middle.

In a large bowl, combine the tomatoes, onion, beans, garlic, basil, vinegar, and a pinch of salt. Let the mixture rest for 30 minutes.

To make the vinaigrette, drain the juice that's formed at the bottom of the tomato bowl and transfer it to a small bowl. Whisk in the ¼ cup oil.

When you're ready to serve, remove the garlic cloves from the tomato mixture and add the toasted bread cubes. Pour on the vinaigrette and toss everything together. Add a little more salt if needed. Let sit for a few minutes before serving.

KITCHEN NOTES: When I make panzanella, I prefer to use a crusty sourdough bread. Because of the fermentation process used to make it, sourdough is more digestible than some other gluten-containing breads. As I've said before, though, use the type of bread that works best for you.

Kale Avocado Salad

MAKES 2-3 SERVINGS

Pantry Essential: **NATURAL SWEETENER**

Kale is a pretty hearty green that lends itself well to soups and sautéing. But when it comes to eating it raw, it can be tough to chew. Literally. The key to making kale work well in salads is to cut the greens super thin into small ribbons or chop it very fine. This makes it easier to eat and more welcoming to leafy-green newbies. Massaging the avocado and honey into the greens makes it even easier. Don't be shy to add a handful of other veggies—more peppers, cabbage, or cucumbers would make nice additions.

1 avocado

2 teaspoons raw honey

Juice of 1 small lemon, or to taste

Sea salt

5 cups lacinato (dinosaur) kale, thinly sliced into ribbons

1 red bell pepper, diced

Mash the avocado, honey, lemon, and a pinch of salt together in a small bowl.

In a large bowl, combine the kale and bell pepper, then add the avocado mixture with your hands. Massage the avocado mixture into the kale and peppers for about 3 minutes or until the kale softens and turns bright green. Add more salt to taste. Add more lemon juice if needed. Serve pronto.

KITCHEN NOTES: Yes, it might seem crazy to put your hands into the salad. But just get a little dirty with this one. It's worth it!

Carrot and Pistachio Salad

MAKES 2-4 SERVINGS

Pantry Essentials: **NUTS, NATURAL SWEETENER**

Can you like a salad just because it's pretty? I mean, this salad also tastes good...but it sure is pretty. It's got gorgeous orange carrot ribbons, the fresh herbs, and the little pale green pistachios. I'm not a fan of super-sweet salads, so I went pretty light with the maple syrup on the nuts. If you want a little more a sweetness, you can double the amount of maple syrup.

¾ cup raw shelled pistachios

1 tablespoon real maple syrup

Sea salt

3 tablespoons canned full-fat coconut milk

1 tablespoon apple cider vinegar, or to taste

1 tablespoon olive oil

1 teaspoon raw honey (or maple syrup if you don't do honey)

1 tablespoon fresh lime juice, or to taste

5 carrots, shaved into ribbons

Handful of your favorite herb or herbs
(I like mint and dill together)

Preheat the oven to 350 and line a baking sheet with parchment paper.

Combine the pistachios, maple syrup, and a pinch of salt. Spread them on the baking sheet and bake for 8 to 10 minutes, until they're nice and brown. Set them aside to cool.

To make the dressing, whisk together the coconut milk and apple cider vinegar. Set it aside for 10 minutes and then whisk in the oil, honey, lime juice, and a pinch of salt. Taste and add more lime juice, vinegar, or salt if needed.

In a large bowl, toss the carrots, pistachios, and herbs together with the dressing. Use your hands to really dig in there and get everything blended together. Serve.

Jerusalem Salad

MAKES 3-4 SERVINGS

Pantry Essential: **TAHINI**

I judge Middle Eastern restaurants not on their hummus or even the service, but on their Jerusalem salad. I don't want it too soupy, but I don't want it lacking in tahini and lemon juice, either. I also don't want random lettuces in there, but I do want lots of parsley! I'm picky, I know. My version gives me everything I need in the perfect ratios. That said, if you're a soupy fan, make it soupier. And if you love those random lettuces, add those, too. No shame in making it just the way you like it!

**1 large cucumber, chopped
(you can decide if you want to peel or not)**

1 pint cherry or grape tomatoes, quartered

⅓ cup Italian chopped parsley

¼ cup tahini

¼ cup fresh lemon juice

3 tablespoons water

Dash of cayenne (optional)

Pinch of sea salt

In a large bowl, combine the cucumber, tomatoes, and parsley. Make the dressing in a small bowl by mixing together the tahini, lemon juice, water, cayenne, and salt. Add more of whatever you think it needs. Pour the dressing over the veggies and toss it all together. Serve.

Daniel Holzman's Chopped Vegetable Salad

MAKES 2-4 SERVINGS

Pantry Essential: **TAHINI**

When you ask one of the owners of the Meatball Shop to create a plant-based recipe for your cookbook, you're not exactly sure what his response will be. But then he says yes (cool!) and sends you his recipe (a salad?), and your mind is blown.

Yes, Daniel Holzman is the co-owner of NYC's popular restaurant chain known for all things meat and cheese, but he's a huge veggie lover, too. His approach to food is the perfect example of what this book is all about—it doesn't have to be all or nothing when it comes to your diet. This recipe has a lot of veggies going on. A lot. If you don't have a specific veggie here, that's OK. Daniel said it's a great way to use leftover veggies, and whatever you have on hand will probably work great.

FOR THE DRESSING:

2 teaspoons unseasoned rice vinegar

1 tablespoon tahini

3 tablespoons raw (untoasted) sesame oil

1 tablespoon Braggs liquid amino acid

Juice of 1 lemon

FOR THE SALAD:

1 small tomato, diced (about 1 cup)

20 or so snap peas, diced (about 1 cup)

½ endive, diced (about ½ cup)

4 radishes, diced (about ½ cup)

¼ head radicchio, diced (about 1 cup)

1 small carrot, diced (about 1 cup)

¼ cup roughly chopped parsley

⅓ cucumber, roughly peeled and diced (about 1 cup)

1 cup chopped broccoli (include small pieces of stem along with florets)

10 mint leaves, diced

2 green onions, thinly sliced

1 cup cooked chickpeas (garbanzos), drained and rinsed if canned

2 pinches of sea salt

To make the dressing: Whisk all of the ingredients together. It takes a little energy to break up the tahini, so you can use a blender if you prefer.

To make the salad: In a large bowl, mix together all of the chopped vegetables, the herbs, and the chickpeas. Pour on the dressing, add the salt, and toss to coat. You can eat this salad immediately or let it macerate in the fridge for a couple hours or up to overnight.

Quinoa Taco Salad

MAKES 4 SERVINGS

Pantry Essential: **BEANS, SEEDS**

The first time I had quinoa, I was pretty mad about it. I'd scooped a giant spoonful of plain unseasoned quinoa onto my plate from a salad bar. It was bland and boring, and I just didn't understand all the rage about this little seed. As I began to learn how to cook, I realized something BIG: quinoa really shines when it's got friends—spices, herbs, and veggies. I invited the whole gang over for this one and threw in some tortilla chips for a little added crunch and texture.

½ teaspoon cumin

½ teaspoon chili powder

¼ cup fresh lime juice, or to taste

2 cups cooked quinoa, room temperature (not hot)

½ small onion, minced

1 cup cherry tomatoes, quartered

¼ cup chopped cilantro

1 cup cooked black beans, drained and rinsed if canned

Sea salt

1 avocado, diced

Hot sauce

Sprouted or regular tortilla chips

In a small bowl, mix the cumin, chili powder, and lime juice and set it aside.

In a large bowl, combine the quinoa, onion, tomatoes, cilantro, and black beans. Gently stir in the spiced lime juice and toss to coat. Add a pinch of salt. Taste and add more lime juice and salt if needed. Before serving, top the salad with avocado and hot sauce (that step is crucial) and then add a handful of tortilla chips in the bowl or crushed on top.

KITCHEN NOTES: Make sure to freshen up leftovers with a squeeze or two of lime juice.

Tomato and Corn Salad with Jalapeño-Lime Dressing

MAKES 4 SERVINGS

Pantry Essential: **NATURAL SWEETENER**

During the summer, I try to figure out as many ways as possible to eat tomatoes and corn together. This salad is one of my favorite ways to do that. It's really fresh and light, but has a nice kick from the jalapeño and lime. The oil is optional—I tend to like the veggies just as they are, but for some people, the oil adds another layer of richness. If you're going to use it, I highly recommend using a good-quality olive oil (see page 37 for more information on how to find one).

½ large jalapeño, seeded and chopped (about 2 tablespoons)

¼ cup fresh lime juice

½ teaspoon raw honey (or maple syrup if you don't do honey)

2 teaspoons olive oil (optional)

Sea salt

Kernels from 3 large ears boiled or grilled corn

1 pint cherry or grape tomatoes, cut in half

5–7 large basil leaves, torn

In a small bowl, mix together the jalapeño, lime juice, honey, oil (if you're using it), and a pinch of salt. Let the dressing rest for 5 minutes.

In a large bowl, combine the corn, tomatoes, and basil.

Pour the dressing over the salad and toss it all together. Serve.

Creamy Millet Salad

MAKES 4 SERVINGS

Pantry Essentials: **COCONUT, GRAIN**

I eat a lot of sauerkraut, and I always seem to have a couple jars floating around the fridge. Most don't even have any kraut left in them; they're just empty jars with the juice. It always felt so wasteful to throw away all that juice. I knew at some point I'd find a way to use it...and this salad dressing is it! The juice works the same way a vinegar would—it provides a zesty punch. So next time you've polished off your jar of sauerkraut, be sure to save the juice.

FOR THE DRESSING:

½ cup canned full-fat coconut milk

1 small garlic clove

3 tablespoons sauerkraut juice

2 tablespoons chopped fresh dill

Pinch of sea salt

FOR THE REST:

2 cups cooked millet

1 cup favorite greens (spinach, kale, or chard), diced very small, or microgreens

1 large avocado, cut into cubes

2–3 tablespoons fresh lemon juice

Sea salt

Combine all the dressing ingredients in a high-speed blender and blend until the mixture is smooth and green. Set it aside.

In a large bowl, combine the millet, greens, and avocado. Pour the dressing over the salad and toss gently to coat. Add 2 tablespoons of the lemon juice. Taste and add more lemon juice and salt as needed.

KITCHEN NOTES: If sauerkraut is not already in your regular rotation, I encourage you to give it a shot. Because it's fermented, it contains powerful probiotics that promote digestive health (I love eating a scoop in the morning as a way to help keep me regular). The most tasty and most beneficial sauerkraut can be found in the refrigerated section of the grocery store. I'm a huge fan of Bubbies and Farmhouse Culture.

Pomegranate, Spinach, and Walnut Salad

MAKES 2-4 SERVINGS

Pantry Essentials: **NUTS, NATURAL SWEETENER**

Pomegranates can be an intimidating fruit. What are those little alien seeds? How do you get them out? No, seriously. How do you get them out? I was intimidated the first time I bought one, too. But it turns out it's really not that hard to remove the seeds—you just need a little patience and a method that actually works.

If you've already got your method nailed, by all means, get started on this recipe. But if you need help, it's homework time! Hop online and watch a few videos on how to get the seeds out of a pomegranate. You'll find a few techniques that are pretty consistent (personally, I'm a fan of the submerging-in-water technique). See which one you think looks most doable and try it.

Yes, the pomegranate seeds and vinegar add the perfect amount of sweet and tart to this salad. But what I *really* love about it is how easy it is to make. Since everything goes into one big bowl, there's very little cleanup...and that always makes a dish a winner to me.

1 cup pomegranate seeds

1 tablespoon chopped fresh mint

1 tablespoon fresh lime juice, or to taste

2 teaspoons real maple syrup, or to taste

2 teaspoons apple cider vinegar

Pinch of sea salt

5 cups spinach, chopped

¾ cup walnuts, toasted

In a large bowl, combine the pomegranate, mint, lime juice, maple, vinegar, and salt; let sit for about 10 minutes. Add the spinach and walnuts, and toss everything together. Using your hands works best here. Add more salt, lime juice, or sweetener if needed.

Red Lentil Soup

MAKES 4-6 SERVINGS

Pantry Essentials: **TAMARI, LENTILS, VEGGIE BROTH**

As much as I try to shop smart and not waste food, sometimes I just can't get to those couple stalks of celery at the bottom of my produce drawer before they go bad or find a use for that poor single tomato on my counter that's about to turn to mush. This soup is a perfect remedy to clear my plant conscience and not let any of my lone produce go to waste. With just a few veggies and a handful of pantry essentials, you'll have a quick and healthy dinner as well as leftovers for lunch the next day.

Olive or coconut oil

1 onion, diced

2 garlic cloves, diced

2 carrots, diced

2 celery stalks, diced

1 large tomato, diced

1 teaspoon cumin

2 teaspoons tamari or coconut aminos

Sea salt

4 cups veggie broth or water
(I used 2 cups of each)

1 cup red lentils

Juice of 1 small lemon

Pepper

Handful of cilantro (optional)

In a medium pot, heat a glug of oil over medium heat. When it's hot, add the onion and sauté for 5 to 7 minutes, until it's soft and translucent. Add the garlic, carrots, celery, tomato, cumin, tamari, and a pinch of salt, and cook until the veggies become soft. Add the broth and lentils. Bring the mixture to a boil and then reduce heat to low. Cover and simmer the soup for 30 minutes, stirring a few times.

Transfer half of the soup to a high-speed blender and blend until it's smooth. Pour it back into the pot and stir in the lemon juice. Salt and pepper to taste. Garnish with chopped cilantro if you like.

Notes from the Field: Nobody's Perfect

———

A few winters ago, I found myself sobbing on the bathroom floor. Not a pretty cry. The kind that sounds bad and looks even worse. Before I changed my diet, crying in the bathroom was a weekly occurrence. But it had been a while since I had been that upset, and I didn't like that the feeling was back.

Pretty soon, my husband knocked on the door and asked if he could come in. He sat down next to me and asked what was going on. I rattled off a list of complaints that involved working too much and traveling for the holidays and being stressed about work, but none of these things should have made me feel as bad as I did.

And then he asked me the most important question—he asked if I had been taking care of myself. REALLY? I was so annoyed. *Of course* I was taking care of myself. I had made it *my job* to take care of myself.

But the more I thought about it, the more I realized that the real answer was NO. It had been three days since I'd had my favorite smoothie. I hadn't been eating enough, and when I did eat, I opted for a spoonful of nut butter in front of the fridge. I was so crazy with work and trying to help other people that I had forgotten to take care of myself.

Sometimes you have to go off course to see how much you can feel the effects of real food. I'd never doubted what I was doing, but I'd also never really recognized just how powerful it was: even though life could get a little wacky, I had this awesome safety net to keep me feeling great. That made me cry even more, happy tears this time.

As you begin to eat more plants, it's OK to not be perfect. One day of no plants doesn't have to turn into a whole week. Just jump back in and keep going. One meal can make all the difference in your day.

Easy Spicy Miso Soup

MAKES 2-3 SERVINGS

Pantry Essential: **TAMARI**

When we were shooting this recipe, our incredible photographer, Nicole, read the title and said, "Isn't all miso soup EASY?" Uh, yeah, maybe she was right. But the reason I used *easy* in the title is because if you've never cooked with miso, it can be intimidating. I promise you it's not. This soup comes together really quickly and is perfect for a night when you just don't feel like cooking a big meal.

If you're allergic to soy (miso is fermented soy), Miso Master makes a soy-free chickpea version.

4 cups water

4–5 shiitake mushrooms,
chopped into bite-size pieces

3 tablespoons miso paste (yellow, white, or red)

1 head baby bok choy,
trimmed and chopped into bite-size pieces

1 sheet nori (dried seaweed),
torn into 1-inch squares

1 green onion, diced

2 teaspoons tamari or coconut aminos

Dash of cayenne

In a medium pot, combine the water and mushrooms and bring them to a boil. Turn the heat to low to stop the boil and add the miso. Stir until the miso dissolves completely. Stir in the bok choy, nori, onion, tamari, and cayenne. Remove the pot from the heat and let it sit for 2 or 3 minutes. Serve.

KITCHEN NOTES: Once you've got the hang of how to make this easy miso soup, add your own spin—ginger, chili oil, noodles, or more sea veggies.

Roasted Cauliflower and Fennel Soup

MAKES 4–6 SERVINGS

Pantry Essential: **NUTS**

As you might have gathered, I like to keep things simple in the kitchen. This means that I do my best to minimize the use of dishes, baking sheets, and gear for each recipe (read: I don't really like doing dishes). In this recipe, I roast the cauliflower and fennel on the same baking sheet and eliminate the need to wash another pan. If you don't care about doing more dishes and want to roast them separately, just line another sheet with parchment paper and follow the cooking times below. You'll still end up with a creamy, dreamy soup that's tasty any time of year.

1 medium cauliflower, cut into florets

Olive oil

Sea salt and pepper

1 fennel bulb, fronds trimmed and discarded, sliced

½ cup raw cashews, soaked for at least a couple hours (overnight is best), drained

3 cups veggie broth, plus more if needed

Olive, coconut, or grape seed oil, if desired for sautéing

1 medium onion, diced

2 garlic cloves, diced

Preheat the oven to 425 degrees. Line a large baking sheet with parchment paper.

Toss the cauliflower with a little olive oil, salt, and pepper. Do the same with the fennel. Spread cauliflower on one end of the baking sheet and the fennel on the other. Roast them for 10 minutes, then turn the veggies with a spatula. After 20 minutes, check to see if the fennel is soft and has browned a little on the edge. It should be ready, but it might need more time. When it's ready, remove the pan from the oven, transfer the fennel to a bowl or plate, and set it aside.

With a spatula, spread the cauliflower out over the whole pan and roast it for another 5 to 10 minutes, until it is also soft and browned on the edges. When it's finished cooking, set a few florets aside to use for garnish.

While the cauliflower is roasting, add the cashews and 1 cup of the veggie broth to a high-speed blender and blend until the mixture is completely smooth. This might take up to 5 minutes, depending on the speed and power of your blender. Leave the cashew

KITCHEN NOTES: I usually serve this soup straight from the blender. But if you'd like it to be hotter, transfer everything from the blender into a pot and bring it to a low simmer on the stove before serving.

mixture in the blender. You'll be adding the rest of the ingredients soon.

Heat a little glug of olive or grape seed oil or a couple tablespoons of veggie broth in a pan and place it over medium heat. When the pan is hot, add the onion and sauté until the pieces are soft and translucent, 5 to 7 minutes. Add the garlic and sauté for a few more minutes. Add the remaining 2 cups veggie broth and heat for a couple minutes.

Working in batches, if necessary, transfer the contents of the pan, the cauliflower, and the fennel to the blender with the blended cashews. Blend until the mixture is smooth, or to your desired consistency. Add more veggie broth if needed and add salt and pepper to taste. Serve with reserved cauliflower florets on top.

Roasted Potato, Corn, and Leek Chowder

MAKES 4-6 SERVINGS

Pantry Essentials: **COCONUT, VEGGIE BROTH**

This soup makes me happy. It just does. It was the first recipe I made for this book (successfully), and it holds a special place in my heart. It doesn't require too many ingredients and tastes so rich and comforting that you'll have a hard time believing it doesn't contain any cream.

I like serving this soup at room temperature. If you want it piping hot, just throw it back on the stove after it's blended.

2 medium potatoes, cut into 1-inch cubes (I like Yukon golds)

Olive or coconut oil

Sea salt and pepper

2 cups sliced leeks (about 3 leeks), or 1 medium yellow onion, chopped

Kernels from 3 ears cooked corn

2 garlic cloves, chopped

1 cup canned full-fat coconut milk

2 cups veggie broth, plus more if needed

KITCHEN NOTE: If you're eating this the next day, make sure to stir in a little veggie broth while heating it up to get it back to the original consistency.

Preheat the oven to 425 degrees and line a baking sheet with parchment paper. Toss the potatoes with a little olive or melted coconut oil and salt and pepper. Roast them on the baking sheet until they are slightly browned, about 40 minutes.

Meanwhile, place a large skillet over medium heat and add a glug of oil or veggie broth. When the pan is hot, add the leeks and sauté until they're soft, about 5 minutes. Add the corn and garlic and sauté for another 3 to 5 minutes. Scoop out about ⅓ cup of the sautéed mixture and set it aside. Add the coconut milk to the skillet and simmer for another 5 minutes.

When the potatoes are ready, transfer ⅓ cup of them to the reserved sautéed mixture.

Transfer the remaining potatoes, the coconut milk mixture, and the veggie broth to a high-speed blender and blend until smooth. Add more veggie broth, if you prefer; I like serving this soup a little thick. Salt to taste.

When you're ready to serve, transfer the soup to individual bowls and garnish with a little of the reserved potato, corn, and leek mixture on top to fancy it up.

Thai Coconut Soup

MAKES 4 SERVINGS

Pantry Essentials: **VEGGIE BROTH, COCONUT**

The beauty of this soup is that it will take you less time to make than it would to have it delivered from your favorite local Thai restaurant. I love serving it with a little cooked rice thrown into each bowl at the end to make a heartier meal, but it tastes just as good without.

4 cups veggie broth

1 (14-ounce) can full-fat coconut milk

1-inch piece of fresh ginger, peeled

2 lemongrass stalks, peeled and smashed with the flat of a knife or rolling pin

1 red Thai chili, seeded and sliced

2 garlic cloves, smashed with the flat of a knife

8 ounces mushrooms (shiitake, button, or a mix), sliced

¼ cup fresh lime juice

1 tablespoon real maple syrup

2 tablespoons tamari or coconut aminos

2 cups cooked rice (optional)

Handful of cilantro (optional)

In a large pot, bring the veggie broth to a boil. Lower the heat and add the coconut milk, ginger, lemongrass, chili, and garlic. Cover and simmer for 10 minutes.

Strain the soup through a colander or sieve into another pot. Discard the ginger, garlic, and lemongrass. I like to reserve the chili slices to use as garnish at the end.

Add the mushrooms, lime juice, maple syrup, and tamari and lightly simmer for another few minutes, until the mushrooms soften. To serve, spoon a little rice into each bowl (if you like), ladle the soup on top, and garnish with chilies and some cilantro, if desired.

TASTERS TELL ALL...

"I used a slotted spoon to remove the lemongrass, ginger, and garlic from the pot, rather than strain the soup, and it worked great!"

Creamy Roasted Tomato Soup

MAKES 4-6 SERVINGS

Pantry Essentials: **NUTS, VEGGIE BROTH**

This soup is a perfect way to use all of those beautiful tomatoes that pop up at the market and grocery store in the summer months. Fresh, ripe, in-season tomatoes really make this soup shine. Don't be afraid to buy the funky, misshapen heirloom varieties that you see at the market—those ugly ducklings are sometimes the most delicious.

4 medium tomatoes, cored and cut into quarters

4 large garlic cloves, smashed with the flat of a knife

Olive oil

2 onions, cut in half and thinly sliced

½ cup raw cashews, soaked for a few hours (overnight is best), drained

1 cup veggie broth, plus more if needed

1 tablespoon tomato paste

Sea salt and pepper

Preheat the oven to 400 degrees. Place the tomatoes and garlic in a baking dish and roast them for 40 minutes.

In a medium skillet (choose one you have a lid for), heat a glug of oil or veggie broth on medium. When the pan is hot, sauté the onions for 5 to 7 minutes, until the pieces are translucent.

While the onions are cooking, whiz the cashews with 1 cup veggie broth and the tomato paste in a high-speed blender until the mixture is completely smooth. Depending on the speed of your blender, this could take up to 5 minutes. (Don't worry about cleaning your blender when you're done—everything will be going back in there soon.)

Pour the cashew mixture into the pan with the onions and cover it. Simmer the mixture over low heat for 5 minutes, stirring once.

Transfer the onion mixture and the roasted tomatoes to the blender and blend until it's smooth. If you have a small blender, do this in batches. This is a pretty thick soup, so add more veggie broth if you wish. Add salt and pepper to taste.

You can serve this immediately or, if you prefer it piping hot, put it back on the stove and reheat it.

Serve it with a sprinkle of salt and a drizzle of olive oil.

Ruth Reichl's Butternut Squash Soup

MAKES 4-6 SERVINGS

Pantry Essential: SEEDS

I'm not easily starstruck. I've never asked a celebrity for an autograph, wanted a selfie, or freaked out just seeing someone walk down the street. I've always felt that famous people are normal humans who happen to have jobs that require the rest of us to know their faces.

That said, there are a handful of people I would be nervous to meet. Here's a short list: Julius Erving (a.k.a. Dr. J, my all-time favorite basketball player), Paul Rand (the late great graphic designer), and Ruth Reichl (former *Gourmet* magazine editor and *New York Times* best-selling author). So when Ruth agreed to contribute one of her recipes to my book...I was speechless. Well, actually, one four-letter word came out of my mouth, pretty loudly. She's one of my queens when it comes to food, and I'm beyond grateful to have her delicious and simple butternut squash soup recipe in this book.

1 onion

1 stalk celery

2 carrots

Olive oil

1-pound butternut squash

½ pound waxy potatoes (Yukon golds are good)

Sea salt

2½ cups boiling water

Pumpkin seed oil

Toasted pumpkin seeds

Diced apples (optional)

Begin by coarsely chopping the onion, celery, and carrots; you don't have to be fussy about this since you're going to end up pureeing everything. Slick the bottom of a casserole or Dutch oven with olive oil, add the vegetables, and let them tumble into tenderness, which should take about 10 minutes.

Peel the butternut squash and cut it into ¾-inch or so cubes. Peel the potatoes and cut them into chunks of the same size. Stir them into the vegetables in the casserole, add a couple teaspoons of sea salt and the boiling water, cover, and simmer until everything is very soft. This will take about half an hour.

Very carefully puree the soup in a blender, in small batches, making sure the top of the blender is secure (hot soup can be painful).

Taste for seasoning and serve the soup drizzled with a few drops of pumpkin seed oil and a sprinkle of toasted pumpkin seeds. A crisp dice of apples on top makes this look lovely and adds a very pleasing note of sweetness.

Most squashes are dull creatures, workhorse vegetables you eat because you know you should. Butternut, on the other hand, is a sensual vegetable that lures you in with its lavish color and then seduces you with its luxurious texture. This deceptively simple soup uses every bit of butternut's potential, turning a handful of ingredients into one of the most satisfying soups you'll ever eat.

7 | Mains

ROASTED ASPARAGUS AND TOMATO PASTA

OPEN-FACED FALAFEL SANDWICH

MEXICAN FRIED RICE NACHOS

SAAG PLANT-NEER

CREAMY BUTTERNUT SQUASH AND LENTIL TACOS

JOHNNY MARZETTI REMIX

COCONUT QUINOA AND BEANS

EASY RED CURRY VEGGIE BOWLS

PERRY HENDRIX'S ROASTED CARROTS AND SPROUTED LENTIL TABBOULEH

GO-TO SPAGHETTI MARINARA

BLACK-EYED PEAS AND GREENS

CREAMY MUSHROOM LASAGNA

MASHED POTATO AND GRAVY BOWL

CORN CAKES WITH BLACK BEAN SPREAD

ZA'ATAR SWEET POTATOES AND GARLICKY KALE

WHITE BEAN PEPPER CHILI

SPICY BROCCOLI RICE

Roasted Asparagus and Tomato Pasta

MAKES 2-4 SERVINGS

Pantry Essential: **NUTRITIONAL YEAST**

If you're new to gluten-free pasta, this is a great recipe to get you started. Because the veggies and basil are the stars of the show, you can't really go wrong with your choice of pasta (think of the pasta as backup dancers). I've made this recipe with mung bean, chickpea, and brown rice pasta, and they all worked great!

I also encourage you to play with the finishing touches to get them just right for you in terms of heat and saltiness. I tend to go a little wild with the red pepper and nutritional yeast, but I've left the measurements open for you to do your thing.

1 large bunch asparagus (shoot for around 40 medium-thick stalks), washed and trimmed

Good-quality olive oil

Sea salt

16 ounces gluten-free pasta of your choice

2 cups cherry tomatoes, quartered

12 basil leaves

Red pepper flakes

Nutritional yeast

Preheat the oven to 400 degrees and line a baking sheet with parchment paper.

Cut the asparagus spears into thirds and toss them with a little bit of olive oil and salt. Transfer them to the prepared baking sheet and roast for 10 to 15 minutes, or until the spears are bright green and fork-tender.

While the asparagus is roasting, cook the pasta according to the package instructions. (I like to try to coordinate the pasta and asparagus to finish right around the same time, so I can toss them together warm.)

Combine the roasted asparagus, pasta, tomatoes, and basil. Drizzle on a glug or two of olive oil and add a few pinches of red pepper flakes, a couple shakes of nutritional yeast, and some salt. Taste and season again as desired. Serve.

Open-Faced Falafel Sandwich

MAKES 4-5 SANDWICHES

Pantry Essential: LEGUMES

After reading this recipe, you might be thinking, *Um, can't I just use canned chickpeas?* You certainly can try. I just don't love the texture as much and prefer using dried ones soaked overnight when making falafel. Canned chickpeas will make your dough a little wetter and harder to work with. That said, you know I'm all about experimentation and figuring out what works best in your own kitchen, so if all you have on hand are canned chickpeas and you are dying to try this recipe, I say go for it.

I've made this into a sandwich, but it can just as easily be a salad. Ditch the bread and throw everything on top of a bed of greens.

1 cup dried chickpeas (garbanzo beans), soaked overnight and drained

Toppings (choose a few): hummus (page 83), baba ganoush (page 81), chopped cucumber, chopped tomato, sliced red or pickled onions, tahini, lemon juice, hot sauce

⅓ cup chopped red onion

1 large garlic clove, crushed with the flat of a knife

2 tablespoons fresh lemon juice

2 tablespoons good olive oil

1½ teaspoons cumin, or to taste

⅓ cup fresh parsley

⅓ cup fresh dill

Cayenne

Sea salt

½ teaspoon baking soda

Olive or coconut oil for frying

Gluten-free, sprouted, or other bread of your choice

Start by patting the chickpeas dry (you want them as dry as possible): lay them out on a kitchen towel, fold the towel over, pat gently, then let them sit for a few minutes.

Meanwhile, get your toppings ready to go. The falafel tastes best served warm, so make sure whatever you want to use is prepared.

Combine the chickpeas, chopped onion, garlic, lemon juice, olive oil, cumin, herbs, a dash of cayenne, and a large pinch of salt in a food processor and pulse until the mixture is combined, but not super smooth. You want a little grain to it. Add the baking soda and pulse a few times until it's incorporated. Taste and add more salt, cumin, or cayenne if needed.

Form the falafel mixture into patties: scoop up about 1 tablespoon at a time, roll it into a ball, and gently flatten it.

In a skillet, heat a glug of olive oil or scoop of coconut oil over medium-high. Working in batches, place a few falafel patties in the hot skillet and press down gently with the back of the spatula to flatten them a little more, like a pancake. When they begin to brown, about 3 minutes, flip them over and cook the other side until it is browned. Place the cooked falafel on a plate lined with a paper towel.

To assemble the sandwich, spread a generous amount of hummus or baba ganoush on a piece of bread and lay the falafel patties on next. Top with cucumbers, tomatoes, onions, a drizzle of tahini, a pinch of salt, a squeeze of lemon juice, or anything else you wish. Add a little hot sauce, too. Grab a knife and fork and dive in.

Mexican Fried Rice Nachos

MAKES 4-6 SERVINGS

Pantry Essentials: BEANS, GRAINS

This recipe was inspired by a half hour of binge watching fried rice how-to videos. Weird, I know. But have you ever seen fried rice being made by a pro? There's something so mesmerizing about the sound of the sizzling oil, the crazy-fast prep work, and the wok being handled with such finesse and ease. After my viewing party (of one), I was inspired to make fried rice—well, semi-fried—and I threw in some nachos, too.

Olive or coconut oil

1 small onion, chopped

2 garlic cloves, minced

1 jalapeño, seeded and chopped

Pinch of cumin

Sea salt

1 cup cooked black beans, drained and rinsed if canned

Kernels from 2 ears boiled or grilled corn

1 tablespoon fresh lime juice

1 cup cooked jasmine rice

2 teaspoons tamari or coconut aminos

1 bag (6–10 ounces) sprouted or corn tortilla chips

Toppings (choose a few): guacamole, avocado, chopped tomatoes, diced raw onions, cilantro, Cilantro Cream (page 63)

In a large skillet, heat some oil over medium and sauté the onions until they are soft and translucent, 5 to 7 minutes. Add the garlic, jalapeño, cumin, and a pinch of salt and cook for another few minutes. Stir in the black beans and corn. Cook for a few more minutes. Transfer the mixture to a bowl and stir in the lime juice. Set aside.

Drain any excess liquid from the skillet and place it over high. Add a glug of oil. When the pan is hot, add the jasmine rice, after using your hands to break up any clumps. Toss the rice around the pan for about 3 minutes. When you see a few grains browning, pour the bean and corn mixture back into the skillet, add the tamari, and toss everything together until the mixture is combined and piping hot.

On a large plate or baking sheet, spread out the chips and top them with fried rice. Add any toppings you like and serve.

Saag Plant-neer

MAKES 2-4 SERVINGS

Pantry Essentials: **GLUTEN-FREE FLOUR, COCONUT**

Back in the day, I was really picky about trying new cuisines. Indian food was out of the question—too many vegetables, too many spices, and not enough pizza. But as my taste buds have changed, I've become a real fan of Indian food. Sadly, I never got to try real-deal saag paneer ("paneer" is a type of soft cheese) before changing my diet, but in this version I aim to capture the flavors of the classic dish while replacing the cream and cheese with a 100 percent planty "paneer."

FOR THE PANEER:

1 cup chickpea (garbanzo bean) flour

1 tablespoon nutritional yeast

1 teaspoon sea salt

½ cup warm water

Olive or coconut oil

FOR THE SAAG:

1 (10-ounce) bag frozen spinach, thawed and water squeezed out, chopped

A few tablespoons veggie broth

1 medium-large yellow onion, minced

1½-inch knob of fresh ginger, peeled and minced (you're shooting for 1 tablespoon)

4 garlic gloves, minced

½ medium jalapeño, seeded and chopped

1 teaspoon cumin

1½ teaspoons garam masala

½ teaspoon turmeric

1 cup canned full-fat coconut milk

Cooked rice (optional)

Start by making the paneer: In a medium bowl, whisk together the chickpea flour, nutritional yeast, and salt, and then stir in the water. Add a glug of olive or a spoonful of coconut oil to a medium-size pan and place it over medium. Scoop tablespoon-size dollops of the batter into the pan; cook these like little pancakes, flipping them over after they begin to brown on one side. When both sides are slightly brown, let them cool. Slice each piece into 4 to 6 cubes and set aside.

Next the saag: Make sure all of the water is squeezed out of your spinach before you start. In a large pan over medium, heat enough veggie broth to cover the pan. When the pan is hot, sauté the onion until the pieces are soft and translucent, 5 to 7 minutes. Add the ginger, garlic, jalapeño, and spices and let cook for another 5 minutes, stirring a few times. Add a tablespoon of water if you are concerned things are going to burn. Go the full 5 minutes to let the spices do their thing. Add the spinach and cook for another 3 to 5 minutes, stirring occasionally. Add the coconut milk, and—you guessed it—let it simmer on low for another 5 minutes. Add the paneer and continue to simmer just until the paneer is warmed through. Serve as is or with rice.

TASTERS TELL ALL...

"This dish has become a staple in our weekly menu at home. Whenever we run out of chickpea flour, we use brown rice flour instead and it tastes just as great!"

Creamy Butternut Squash and Lentil Tacos

MAKES 10-12 TACOS

Pantry Essentials: **LENTILS, COCONUT**

When it comes to veggies, it's hard to think of one that doesn't taste great wrapped up in a tortilla with avocado and hot sauce. These tacos are no exception. Because the lentils and squash are both pretty soft, I suggest adding some crunch with radishes or jalapeños, sprouts, and definitely some pepitas (a.k.a. pumpkin seeds).

1 medium butternut squash, peeled and cut into cubes (about 4 cups)

2¾ teaspoons cumin

Sea salt and pepper

Olive or coconut oil

¾ cup brown lentils, rinsed (black are fine, too, but they will take longer to cook)

Veggie broth

3 teaspoons tamari or coconut aminos

10–12 corn tortillas

2 tablespoons canned full-fat coconut milk

Juice of 1 small lime, or to taste

Toppings such as avocado, pepitas (pumpkin seeds), diced jalapeños, and hot sauce

Preheat the oven to 400 degrees and line a baking sheet with parchment paper.

Toss the squash with ½ teaspoon of the cumin, salt and pepper to taste, and a little oil. Spread the cubes out on the baking sheet and roast them for 30 to 40 minutes, until they're soft.

Meanwhile, in a small pot, combine the lentils with enough broth to cover them and stir in the tamari and remaining 2¼ teaspoons cumin. Bring the mixture to a boil and then reduce the heat and simmer until the lentils are soft, but still a little firm, 25 to 30 minutes. Make sure to watch the pot and add more broth or water if needed to cover the lentils. Taste them as you go to make sure they don't overcook and get mushy. When they're done, drain any excess liquid that hasn't been absorbed.

When you're almost ready to serve, warm the tortillas. You can wrap 5 or 6 in foil and bake them at 375 for about 10 minutes. If you have a gas range, my favorite way is to throw the tortillas on the flame for 30 to 45 seconds on each side to give them a little char. If you do this, watch your fingers or make sure to use tongs!

Transfer the cooked squash to a food processor fitted with the S blade or to a high-speed blender. Process it with the coconut milk and lime juice until smooth. Taste and add salt or more lime juice if needed.

Assemble the tacos: spread a layer of the creamy squash on a warm tortilla and top it with a scoop of lentils. Add whatever toppings you choose and serve.

KITCHEN NOTES: Butternut squash can be a little tough to cut up into uniform pieces. Luckily for this recipe, it's all going to be blended, so they don't need to be perfect. There is also no shame in buying precut squash (I do it a lot). Just make sure you stick to fresh squash for this recipe and not frozen.

You'll likely have leftover lentils, depending on what kind of lentils you use. Store them in the fridge for up to a week and toss them into salads or mix them with roasted veggies.

Johnny Marzetti Remix

MAKES 6 SERVINGS

Pantry Essentials: **LENTILS, NUTS, VEGGIE BROTH**

As the story goes, the original version of this dish was created by an Italian immigrant named Teresa Marzetti in the 1920s. She named the dish after her brother-in-law and served it at her restaurant, Marzetti's, in Columbus, Ohio. (She later went on to create the popular T. Marzetti brand of salad dressings.)

If you grew up in the Midwest, you've probably tasted more than one version of this. If you have no idea what I'm talking about, imagine a casserole-style pasta dish full of cheese, meat, peppers, and celery. My family served it at every single holiday and family reunion, and at least one random night every week. My mom's recipe didn't agree with my stomach, but it was just so good that I didn't want to give it up. So I created my own bellyache-free version.

8 ounces elbow macaroni
(I like to use a brown rice version)

Olive, grape seed, or coconut oil, or veggie broth for sautéing

1 medium onion, diced

2 garlic cloves, chopped

2 celery stalks, chopped

1 green bell pepper, seeded and diced

1 teaspoon dried oregano

1 cup cooked brown lentils

1 cup raw cashews, soaked for at least a few hours (overnight is best), drained

1 cup veggie broth

1 (28-ounce) can crushed tomatoes

2 tablespoons tomato paste

Sea salt

Cook the noodles according to the package instructions.

In a large skillet, heat a little glug of oil or veggie broth on medium heat. When the skillet is hot, add the onion and sauté until the pieces are soft and translucent, 5 to 7 minutes. Add the garlic, celery, bell pepper, and oregano, and sauté for another 5 minutes, or until the pepper pieces have softened. Add a pinch of salt. Stir in the lentils and, using the back of a fork, smash about half of them into the mixture. You want to create a little bit of texture, but not a mush.

While the vegetables cook, combine the cashews and veggie broth in a high-speed blender and blend until the mixture is completely smooth. This might take a few minutes, depending on the speed and power of your blender.

Stir the cashew cream, crushed tomatoes, and tomato paste into the skillet with the vegetables and lentils. Turn the heat to low, cover, and let the mixture simmer for 10 minutes, stirring once about halfway through. Add the noodles and stir. Add a little more salt to taste. Serve.

Coconut Quinoa and Beans

MAKES 4 SERVINGS

Pantry Essentials: **SEEDS, BEANS, COCONUT**

One of my favorite food memories of all time comes from a trip to Honduras, where I ate the same lunch every single day for a week. I know that part of the joy of traveling is tasting new things at every meal and exploring the intricacies of a new culture. I get it. But I didn't care about any of that because all I wanted was this one delicious dish—coconut rice and beans—made by a woman named Jennilyn.

Every day Jennilyn would set up her makeshift kitchen on the side of the road, and every day a line of people would appear to wait for her rice and beans. The line had a lot do with the deliciousness of her food, but I also think it had a lot to do with how much love she gave every single person she served. This recipe is inspired by her.

1½ cups veggie broth, plus enough for sautéing

1 onion, diced

Sea salt

2 garlic cloves, minced

1 poblano pepper, diced

1½ cups quinoa, rinsed

1 (14-ounce) can full-fat coconut milk

3 cups cooked kidney, pinto, or black beans, drained and rinsed if canned

Toppings: avocado and hot sauce

In a large skillet, heat a few tablespoons of the veggie broth over medium. When the pan is hot, add the onion and a pinch of salt. Sauté until the pieces are soft and translucent, 5 to 7 minutes. Add the garlic and the poblano and cook until fragrant, about 30 seconds to a minute.

Add the quinoa and toast it for a few minutes with the onion mixture. Add the coconut milk, 1½ cups veggie broth, and beans. Turn the heat to high and bring to a boil.

Reduce the heat and simmer on low, covered for about 20 minutes, until all the liquid is absorbed. Add salt to taste. Finish with avocado and hot sauce.

KITCHEN NOTES: I love eating this dish cold on the second day. No need to warm it up. But if you do heat it, add a splash of veggie broth.

Easy Red Curry Veggie Bowls

MAKES 3-4 SERVINGS

Pantry Essentials: **NUT BUTTER, COCONUT, GRAINS**

When you're starting to change your diet, I think it's important to have a couple of dishes you know you can make easily, so you don't have to stress over dinner. This is one of those dishes for me—I probably make it at least once a week, typically on those nights when I have no idea what else to cook or I want use up veggies I have in the fridge. I usually have enough leftovers for lunch the next day. I love a BOGO meal!

Olive, grape seed, or coconut oil, or veggie broth for sautéing

½ large onion, diced

2 garlic cloves, minced

1-inch piece of fresh ginger, peeled and minced

1 (14-ounce) can full-fat coconut milk

3 tablespoons almond butter

1–2 tablespoons red curry paste (depending on how spicy you want it)

1 tablespoon tamari or coconut aminos

1 lime, halved

Sea salt

2–3 cups cooked rice or quinoa

4–6 cups of your favorite sautéed or steamed veggies

Heat a little glug of oil or a couple tablespoons of veggie broth in a large skillet over medium. When the pan is hot, add the onion and sauté until the pieces are soft and translucent, about 5 minutes. Add the garlic and ginger and sauté for another minute, until the mixture is fragrant.

Add the coconut milk and stir. Add the almond butter, curry paste, and tamari. You'll need to use the back of the spoon to break up the nut butter and curry paste so it all mixes fully with the coconut milk. Squeeze in the juice from a lime half. If your curry paste already contains lime juice, you may not want more than this. If needed, squeeze in the other half of the lime.

Turn down the heat to low and simmer the curry for at least 5 minutes, or until it reaches your desired consistency. The longer you simmer, the thicker the sauce will become. Salt to taste before serving the curry over rice or quinoa and veggies.

Perry Hendrix's Roasted Carrots and Sprouted Lentil Tabbouleh

MAKES 4 SERVINGS

Pantry Essentials: **TAHINI, GRAINS, LENTILS, NUTS**

I lived in Chicago for fifteen years, so any time someone I know is traveling there, they ask me for a list of my go-to restaurants. Avec is always at the top of that list. It's my all-time favorite restaurant. Ever. When I changed my diet, I had a really hard time saying good-bye to some of my favorite dishes (there were more than a few tears shed over the focaccia). But lucky for me, they're really great at making plant-based dishes, too.

Perry Hendrix, chef de cuisine at Avec, created this ridiculously beautiful and delicious salad recipe. It's inspired by a traditional tabbouleh—which often contains lots of bulgur with just a bit of parsley and few vegetables. Perry's version stays authentic to the traditional flavors of the Middle East, but is grain-free and heavier on the vegetables, nuts, and seeds.

This recipe calls for sprouted lentils; you can sub in regular cooked lentils if you prefer, but I recommend going the sprouted route if you have the time (the process takes about forty-eight hours).

1 bunch small carrots, peeled

2 teaspoons baharat spice (or substitute a mix of equal parts smoked paprika, cumin, and cinnamon)

3 tablespoons olive oil

Sea salt

¼ cup tahini

2 tablespoons water

1 tablespoon plus 2 teaspoons fresh lemon juice

1 cup sprouted lentils (recipe follows)

1 cup cooked quinoa

½ cup parsley leaves

2 blood oranges, peeled, seeded, and diced

½ cup dill fronds

2 Fresno chilies, thinly sliced

½ cup walnuts, toasted

Set your oven to broil and line a rimmed baking sheet with parchment paper.

Toss the carrots with the baharat, 1 tablespoon of the olive oil, and salt to taste; arrange them on the baking sheet. Broil the carrots for about 8 minutes, or until they are tender and well browned.

In a small bowl, combine the tahini with the water and 2 teaspoons of the lemon juice.

In a large bowl, combine the carrots with the remaining 2 tablespoons oil and 1 tablespoon lemon juice as well as the lentils, quinoa, parsley, oranges, dill, chilies, and walnuts. Mix well. Drizzle the tahini sauce over the top and serve.

Sprouted Lentils

MAKES ABOUT 3 CUPS

Pantry Essential: LENTILS

Soak 1 cup of lentils overnight in water to cover. Drain well and place them in a glass jar, covering the top with cheesecloth. Rinse the lentils twice a day with cold water until they have sprouted, around two days. You'll know they're ready when a little tail has formed on each lentil. If you're using red lentils, they'll have itty-bitty tails. Don't worry if you don't see big ones.

Go-To Spaghetti Marinara

MAKES 6-8 SERVINGS

Pantry Essentials: **GRAINS**

Next time you're at the grocery store, play a little game: try to find a jarred spaghetti sauce that doesn't contain sugar or soy additives. My guess is that you'll find about two (hey, Rao's!). The jarred pasta sauces that don't contain sugar and additives tend to be a little pricey, which is why I generally prefer to make my own marinara sauce at home and save the jarred kind for when I'm short on time (hey, Rao's, again!). I'm a huge basil fan, so I use a lot in this recipe. I think it's a pretty crucial ingredient to bring this sauce together, but left the measurements open in case you're not basil-obsessed like me.

1 tablespoon olive oil

1 medium onion, diced

4 garlic cloves, minced

1 (28-ounce) can diced tomatoes

1 (28-ounce) can crushed tomatoes

1–2 cups loosely packed, roughly chopped basil,

¼ cup dry red wine

Sea salt

Brown rice spaghetti or your favorite gluten-free pasta

Nutritional yeast (optional)

In a large pot, heat the oil over low-medium and add the onion. Cook until the onion pieces are soft and translucent, 5 to 7 minutes. Add the garlic and cook for another minute. Stir in the diced tomatoes with their juice. Cover and let the mixture simmer for 15 minutes. Add the other can of tomatoes, the basil, and the wine. Simmer the sauce uncovered for another 15 minutes. Taste and add salt or more basil if needed.

Prepare the pasta according to the package instructions.

Divvy up the pasta into bowls, pour on the sauce, and add a sprinkle of nutritional yeast if you like.

TASTERS TELL ALL...

"I was pleasantly surprised that I didn't need to use a food processor or any equipment, so the dishes were kept to a minimum—perfect for a weeknight meal. I got a couple dinners out of this sauce—first night I used it for the pasta, and the next night I used it for pizza!"

Black-Eyed Peas and Greens

MAKES 4 SERVINGS

Pantry Essentials: **BEANS, VEGGIE BROTH**

This dish is inspired by my move to Charleston, South Carolina. It's actually something I used to make in Chicago, but collard greens grow like weeds down here, and so I've been making it a lot more these days. Every time I see collards at the farmers' market, I still make audible sounds of disbelief at their size. I'm not exaggerating when I say they're as big as your head! Whether you're up North, down South, or all the way on the West Coast—this dish has a sharp, salty, vinegary taste that will keep you coming back for more.

Olive, grape seed, or coconut oil

1 medium onion, chopped

3 garlic cloves, minced

2 celery stalks, chopped

1 medium carrot, chopped

1 jalapeño, seeded and diced

5 cups vegetable broth

1 cup dry black-eyed peas, soaked overnight, rinsed, and drained (about 3 cups after soaking)

1 bay leaf

½ cup apple cider vinegar

2 large collard leaves, destemmed and torn into pieces

Sea salt and pepper

Cooked rice (optional)

In a large pan, add a glug of oil and heat it over medium-low. When the pan is hot, add the onion and cook for 5 to 7 minutes, until it's translucent. Add the garlic, celery, carrot, and jalapeño and cook for another 5 minutes, until the vegetables soften. Add the broth, black-eyed peas, and bay leaf, and bring the mixture to a boil. Lower the heat, cover the pot, and simmer for 20 minutes. Stir in the vinegar and collards. Simmer for another 25 minutes to let the flavors meld. Add salt and pepper to taste. Serve the black-eyed peas over rice if you wish.

Creamy Mushroom Lasagna

MAKES 8 SERVINGS

Pantry Essentials: **NUTS, TAMARI, VEGGIE BROTH**

I've definitely enjoyed some pretty great plant-based lasagnas at restaurants where the chef swaps in vegetables for the noodles. But when I make lasagna at home, I want it to be as close as possible to the kind I grew up with. It has to be saucy and hearty. It has to spend some serious time in the oven. And, most important, it has to have noodles! This recipe checks all of those boxes and is just as delicious as the "real thing."

Olive, grape seed, or coconut oil, or veggie broth for sautéing

3 garlic cloves, minced

16 ounces mushrooms, chopped (you can use a mix of different mushrooms)

1 tablespoon tamari or coconut aminos

1 teaspoon dried thyme

¾ cup raw cashews, soaked for a few hours (overnight is best), drained

1 cup veggie broth

2 big handfuls spinach

10 ounces gluten-free lasagna noodles (I use Tinkyada's brown rice version)

4 cups marinara sauce, store-bought (a 32 oz jar) or homemade (page 152)

Nutritional yeast (optional)

Preheat the oven to 350 degrees.

In a large skillet, heat a glug of oil or veggie broth over medium. When the pan is hot, add the garlic and sauté until it becomes fragrant. This will take about a minute. Add the mushrooms, tamari, and thyme. Cook, stirring every minute or so, for 6 to 8 minutes or until the mushrooms release their water and a little broth starts to form.

Combine the cashews and veggie broth in a high-speed blender and blend until the mixture is completely smooth. This might take up to 5 minutes, depending on the speed and power of your blender. Pour the cashew sauce into the pan with the mushrooms. Reduce the heat to medium-low and simmer for a couple minutes to let the sauce thicken, stirring frequently. Throw in the spinach and stir for another minute.

Prepare the lasagna noodles according to the package instructions. Make sure to do this after your mushroom sauce is ready to go, so the noodles don't sit for too long and start sticking together.

Spread a third of the marinara sauce on the bottom of an 8-by-11-inch baking dish. Add a layer of noodles. Cover the noodles with half of the mushroom cream. Add a layer of noodles. Use another third of the marinara to cover these noodles. Add the remaining mushroom cream. Add the last layer of noodles and cover it with the remaining marinara sauce.

Cover the lasagna with aluminum foil and bake for 30 minutes. Remove the foil, add a sprinkle of nutritional yeast over the top, if you like, and bake for another 15 minutes. Let the lasagna rest for 5 minutes before serving.

Notes from the Field: Being Social

If you decide to truly commit to eating one plant-based meal a day or even go all in and eat three plant-based meals a day, you might find social situations to be challenging at first. I'm going to walk you through a couple of tricks that always work for me.

Out and About

Going out to dinner can feel like an emotional roller coaster in the beginning. If your friends are supportive, they'll survey the menu before you even get a chance to sit down. They'll excitedly point out all the things you can eat. "Look, Jessica! They have salad!" They'll stop the waiter as he's rushing by and scream, "Excuse me! She's VEEEE-GAAAAN. Is there anything she can eat?" Or they'll look at you with sympathy, grab your arm, and say, "Are you OK? Will you be able to find something to eat?"

It's pretty sweet, how much people care about your well-being. But if you're like me, the last thing you want to do is make a big deal or call attention to your food choices in the middle of a restaurant. We just want to eat like everyone else.

To make sure my diet doesn't cause a scene, I always try to choose the restaurant. Whether it's with a client or friends, as soon as the email chain starts shifting to where we should eat, I jump in with three options. I make sure none of these are 100 percent plant-based (unless my dining companions are too). Most important, since I've chosen three places, my dining companions get to weigh in, too. Knowing there will be options for every person's food needs makes it easier on everyone, including the waiter.

Life of the (Dinner) Party

I never like to hurt anyone's feelings. Especially when they've put time and love into preparing food for me. One of the worst experiences I had when I first changed my diet was going to a dinner party and not being able to eat anything the host made. As the rest of the party was diving in, I stared at a few pieces of iceberg lettuce on a salad plate, trying to act like it was the best iceberg lettuce I'd ever had. I could tell my host felt really bad. I kept telling her, "It's OK! I had a huge lunch!" But my stomach was growling so hard, and I couldn't wait to get home to eat.

These days, before I go to any dinner party, I always ask if I can bring something. I don't make a big deal or even mention my dietary needs—I simply say that I'd love to contribute to the meal. Most hosts jump at the chance of delegating a dish or a course to someone else. I make sure that whatever I bring isn't too healthy-looking, and I never introduce a dish by all the things that it's not—announcing your dish is gluten-, dairy-, soy-, and refined-sugar-free is a surefire way to kill the mood with non-planty eaters.

At holidays, my family has put me in charge of the sides. I usually make mashed potatoes and gravy (page 158), some veggies, stuffing (page 103), and Johnny Marzetti (page 146). Which is exactly what we used to eat before I shifted to a plant-based diet. I get to enjoy a meal with my family and celebrate together, and I never feel like the odd man out with my "special" food.

Mashed Potato and Gravy Bowl

MAKES 2-3 SERVINGS (WITH LEFTOVER GRAVY)

Pantry Essentials: **NUTS, VEGGIE BROTH, PLANT-BASED MILK**

Growing up, I remember my pediatrician poking my chubby belly at every visit and saying, "You gotta lay off the mashed potatoes, Jessica." I wasn't a thin kid by any means, but I'm not sure doctors are supposed to fat shame nine-year-olds, either.

Because of him, for the longest time, I thought of mashed potatoes as this insanely "bad," indulgent food. I felt guilty any time I ate them. It wasn't until I changed my diet and created a better relationship with food that I allowed myself to enjoy them without guilt. In celebration of that—and as a sort of "look at me now" to my dear old doc—I've created a whole bowl of them, with greens and gravy, to boot. Eat up, no regret or shame required.

FOR THE GRAVY:

2¾ cups veggie broth, plus enough for sautéing

1 shallot, diced

3 garlic cloves, minced

8 ounces mushrooms, chopped
(I like using baby bellas)

2 teaspoons fresh sage, minced

½ cup dry white wine

½ cup raw cashews, soaked for a few hours
(overnight is best), drained

2 tablespoons tamari or coconut aminos

Sea salt and pepper

FOR THE REST:

2 large potatoes, peeled and quartered
(my favorite is Yukon gold)

Sea salt

1 bunch lacinato kale or favorite green,
chopped (about 6 cups; see Kitchen Notes)

¼–½ cup almond or rice milk

1–2 tablespoons olive or grape seed oil

Pepper

Make the gravy: In a large pan, heat a couple of tablespoons of veggie broth over medium-high. When the pan is hot, add the shallots and garlic and sauté them until they become fragrant, about 30 seconds. Add the mushrooms and sage. Cook for 6 to 8 minutes, until the mushrooms release their water and a little broth starts to form. Stir every minute or so.

Stir in the wine and, using a spoon or spatula, scrape the pan to dissolve the bits of mushrooms and onions stuck to the bottom. Add 2 cups of the broth and let the gravy simmer on low heat for 10 minutes.

While the mushroom mixture is simmering, combine the cashews and the remaining ¾ cup veggie broth in a blender and blend until the mixture is completely smooth. This might take up to 5 minutes, depending on the speed and power of your blender.

When the mushrooms have simmered, pour the cashew cream and tamari into the pan. Let the gravy simmer for another 5 to 8 minutes over low heat until it has thickened. Add a couple pinches of salt and some cracked pepper. Set the gravy aside.

Make the rest: Fill a medium pot with water and add the potatoes. Add a pinch of salt. Turn the heat to high and bring water to a boil, then reduce the heat and simmer the potatoes until they're fork-tender, 15 to 20 minutes.

When you're ready to drain the potatoes, place the chopped greens at the bottom of the colander and pour the hot water over the greens, stopping before the potatoes come out. This will blanch the greens and soften them.

Set the greens aside and finish draining potatoes.

In a medium bowl, mash the potatoes with ¼ cup of the milk and 1 tablespoon of the oil. Add more oil and milk if needed to reach desired consistency, and add salt and pepper to taste.

Place a healthy scoop of mashed potatoes in each bowl. Create a little well in the potatoes with the back of a spoon and fill it with greens. Cover it with mushroom gravy. Serve.

KITCHEN NOTES: If you make this in advance, the gravy will thicken a bit as it sits. When you are ready to serve, heat it with a little veggie broth to get it back to the right consistency.

The blanching method I describe above won't work as well for tougher greens. If you are using heartier greens, like collards or a tougher kale, you will need to sauté or steam them.

TASTERS TELL ALL...

"I cut out dairy recently, and this made me never want to look back. This is my new go-to gravy!"

Corn Cakes with Black Bean Spread

MAKES 4 SERVINGS

Pantry Essentials: **GLUTEN-FREE FLOUR, BEANS**

These little guys are so cute, right? What I most love about them is that you can really do whatever you want for the toppings. I suggest adding something with a little crunch and a touch of heat, too. You can find masa flour at Mexican markets or in the "international" aisle at most grocery stores (it's also starting to pop up in the gluten-free flour/specialty flour section—Bob's Red Mill makes one).

1 cup harina masa flour

Sea salt

¾ cup plus 2 tablespoons warm water

Kernels from 1 large ear boiled or grilled corn (about 1 cup)

1 (15-ounce) can black beans, drained and rinsed, or 1¾ cups cooked beans

2 tablespoons fresh lime juice, or to taste

Olive, grape seed, or coconut oil

Toppings: shredded greens, avocado, hot sauce, salsa, pickled radishes

KITCHEN NOTES: You can spice up this dish by adding a little jalapeño to the black bean spread or the corn cakes.

In a medium bowl, whisk together the masa and ½ teaspoon salt. Slowly stir in all of the warm water until it is combined. Add the corn. You might need to use your hands to work everything together. Cover and set the dough aside for 10 minutes.

Make the black bean spread by combining the beans, lime juice, and a pinch of salt in a food processor. Pulse until the mixture is almost smooth. Taste and add more salt or lime juice if needed.

Divide the dough into eight equal pieces and roll them all into balls. Place a ball between two pieces of parchment paper or plastic wrap. Using the palm of your hand, gently press down to flatten it into a cake about ¼ inch thick. Repeat the process with each ball.

Heat a pan over medium-high. Add a glug of oil. When the pan is hot, add the cakes (you will need to work in batches) and cover with a lid. Flip the cakes after about 3 minutes. Be careful, the corn might pop as the cakes are cooking! They should have some color but will not be completely browned. Replace the lid and cook the other side.

Using a spatula, transfer the corn cakes to a platter. Add a slather of black bean spread, sprinkle on toppings, and serve.

Za'atar Sweet Potatoes and Garlicky Kale

MAKES 2-4 SERVINGS

Pantry Essential: SEEDS

This recipe is in the Mains chapter, but I have to say, I've eaten it at all times of day. It's made it to my breakfast table, and I've definitely whipped it up for a weekend lunch. After I eat it, I always feel so nourished and happy—and my body seems to love me for that. If you're not familiar with za'tar, head back to page 91 and read more about it. The spices are definitely what make this dish so special.

1 tablespoon sesame seeds

1 tablespoon sumac

2 teaspoons dried thyme

¼ teaspoon sea salt

2 medium-size sweet potatoes, cut into cubes (about 4 cups)

Olive oil

3 garlic cloves, chopped

1 bunch kale, destemmed and roughly chopped (about 6 cups)

Sea salt

Preheat the oven to 400 degrees and line a baking with parchment paper.

To make the za'atar, first toast the sesame seeds. In a small dry pan, heat the seeds over medium for 3 to 5 minutes, until they're lightly browned. Stir occasionally, so they don't burn. Let them cool. In a small bowl, combine the sumac, thyme, sesame seeds, and salt.

Fill a medium pot halfway with water and bring it to a boil. Add the sweet potatoes and parboil them (cook them just until they start to soften). This will take 5 to 7 minutes. Drain the potatoes and transfer them to a medium bowl. Toss them with a glug of olive oil and 1 tablespoon of the za'atar seasoning until coated.

Spread the potatoes on the prepared baking sheet and roast them for 10 minutes. Using a spatula, move them around on the baking sheet and continue roasting for another 5 minutes or until they begin to slightly brown.

Mix 1 tablespoon of olive oil into the remaining za'atar and set it aside.

In a large skillet, heat a glug of olive oil over medium. When the pan is hot, add the garlic. Sauté until the garlic becomes fragrant, about a minute. Add the greens and stir until they turn bright green and begin to soften. Add the sweet potatoes and heat everything for a few more minutes.

Top the vegetables with some of the za'atar and oil mixture and serve.

White Bean Pepper Chili

MAKES 6 SERVINGS

Pantry Essential: BEANS

Way before I changed my diet, I made a version of this dish for a chili party I attended every year. Back then, this recipe had a whole bunch of ingredients that I now know were making me pretty sick. After I launched OPP, I went back to the kitchen and created this version, which I could eat without getting a bellyache. This is one of those dishes that tastes even better the next day, making it a perfect lunch to bring to work. I also enjoy spooning it out of a big mug on a cozy Sunday.

Olive, grape seed, or coconut oil, or veggie broth for sautéing

1 medium onion, chopped

1 yellow bell pepper, chopped

1 red bell pepper, chopped

1 poblano pepper, chopped

1 teaspoon chili powder

1 tablespoon tomato paste

1 cup veggie broth

1 (28-ounce) can crushed tomatoes

2 (15-ounce) cans cannellini beans, drained and rinsed, or 3½ cups cooked beans

Juice of 1 lime

¼ teaspoon cayenne

Sea salt

In a large skillet, heat a glug of oil or a few tablespoons of veggie broth over medium. When the skillet is hot, sauté the onion until the pieces turn soft and translucent, 5 to 7 minutes. Add the peppers and cook for another 5 minutes. Add the chili powder and tomato paste and cook for another few minutes. Add the veggie broth. Simmer on low heat and cook until the broth reduces, about 10 minutes. Add the crushed tomatoes and cover the pot, continuing to simmer for 15 minutes. Stir in the beans, lime juice, cayenne, and a giant pinch of salt. Simmer uncovered for at least 10 minutes. Serve the chili as is or with your favorite toppings (a dollop of cashew cream with some chopped onions and jalapeños is the way to go in my house).

TASTERS TELL ALL...

"Peppers are my least favorite vegetable, and I have an embarrassingly low tolerance for spice, but I am very into this chili. The spice was perfect for me, tasty instead of just tasting spicy!"

Spicy Broccoli Rice

MAKES 2–4 SERVINGS

Pantry Essentials: **NUT BUTTER**, **GRAINS**

I think one of the biggest rules of plant-based cooking is to give the same love and attention to the preparation of your veggies that you would to meat, poultry, and fish. We can all agree that plain, steamed, and unseasoned anything isn't super exciting and that's especially true when you're cooking with plants. Sauces are a great way to make your veggie dishes more complex. With the right sauce, you can easily turn a veggie that your family isn't so excited about (in this case, broccoli) into one of their favorites.

¾ cup veggie broth,
plus a little more for sautéing

½ cup natural almond butter

1–2 tablespoons buffalo sauce
(I like Tessemae's)

1 tablespoon fresh lime juice

1 teaspoon tamari or coconut aminos

1 tablespoon real maple syrup

2–3 garlic cloves, chopped

5 cups broccoli florets

Sea salt

2 cups cooked rice (I like short-grain brown rice)
or quinoa

For the sauce, combine ¾ cup veggie broth, the nut butter, buffalo sauce, lime juice, tamari, and maple syrup in a blender and blend until the mixture is smooth. Set it aside.

In a large skillet, heat a glug of veggie broth over medium. When the skillet is hot, add the garlic and sauté until it becomes fragrant and starts to soften, about 30 seconds. Add the broccoli and a pinch of salt. Sauté until the broccoli turns bright green and softens, about 5 minutes.

Add the rice and sauce to the broccoli and stir until the mixture is heated through. Add more veggie broth if you want to make the dish saucier. Taste and add more salt if needed.

KITCHEN NOTES: If you have leftovers, reheat them in a pan with a little veggie broth.

8 | Desserts

ALMOND BUTTER AND BLUEBERRY COOKIES

HONEY PEPPERMINT CUPS

CHOCOLATE MINT COIN COOKIES

DOUBLE CHOCOLATE CUPCAKES WITH SALTED CHIA PUDDING FROSTING

CHOCOLATE HAZELNUT CRISPIES

NUT BUTTER CHOCOLATE TART

ROASTED PINEAPPLE SUNDAES

COCONUT DATE PINWHEELS

TURTLE EGGS

CHOCOLATE CHUNK COOKIES

TRIPLE BERRY SKILLET COBBLER

NO-BAKE TAHINI CHERRY BARS

JULIA TURSHEN'S STRAWBERRY GRANITA WITH WHIPPED COCONUT CREAM

ROASTED BERRY MILKSHAKE

GRASSHOPPER PARFAIT

CRISPY ICE CREAM BARS

How to Melt Chocolate

———

You can easily melt chocolate in the microwave, but I prefer to do it the old-fashioned way—on the stovetop. The best way to do that is to use a double boiler. If you don't have one, that's OK (neither do I). Just follow the instructions below.

Bring a few inches of water to a boil in a small saucepan or pot. Place a nonreactive bowl on top of the pan and check that it fits well: you want to minimize the amount of steam released from the boiling water, and you also don't want the bowl to touch the water. Make sure the bowl and any utensils you are using are dry. Just a little water can stop the chocolate from melting properly.

Add the chocolate to the bowl and stir occasionally until it is melted. Turn off the heat and carefully lift the bowl off the pan. It will be really hot, so make sure to protect your hands!

How to Make Coconut Cream

———

Coconut cream is a staple in plant-based baking and desserts. Simply refrigerate a can of full-fat coconut milk overnight—the liquid and fat will separate, and just like that you'll have the base for coconut cream. Although coconut cream is easy to make, it doesn't work with every brand of coconut milk if certain stabilizers are used. I've done a lot of experimenting, and Thai Kitchen and Native Forest have never let me down.

Once your coconut milk has spent the night in the fridge, carefully remove it. Do not shake the can! You want to make sure you keep the cream separated from the water. Open the can and scoop out the cream that has hardened at the top (use the leftover water for smoothies). With a handheld or stand-up mixer, whip the coconut cream until it is light and fluffy.

Almond Butter and Blueberry Cookies

MAKES 15 COOKIES

Pantry Essentials: **NUT BUTTER, NATURAL SWEETENER, GRAINS, COCONUT**

This is the PB&J of cookies. Well, actually the AB&J (the whole almond butter thing). As you bite into these cookies, you'll get a burst of blueberry paired with the almond butter that's reminiscent of your favorite childhood lunch. These definitely work best with fresh (not frozen) blueberries, so if you can't find fresh blueberries, sub in chocolate chunks instead. I'm sure you're OK with that.

1 cup natural almond butter

2 tablespoons coconut oil, melted

5 tablespoons real maple syrup

1¼ cups rolled oats

¼ teaspoon baking soda

Sea salt, if needed

¾ cup fresh blueberries

Preheat the oven to 350 and line a baking sheet with parchment paper.

In a medium bowl, stir the almond butter, coconut oil, and maple syrup together; if your almond butter is unsalted, add a pinch of salt. Stir in the oats and baking soda. Carefully fold in the blueberries. Do your best keep them whole and not squish them.

Scoop up a tablespoon of dough, roll it into a ball, place it on the parchment paper, and press it down gently with your hand to flatten it a little. Continue placing the cookies on the sheet. They won't spread much, so you can put them pretty close together. Bake the cookies for 10 minutes and then check on them. They should still be slightly soft and doughy to the touch. If they're not there yet, you can bake them a minute or two longer, but you don't want to overbake these. After they've cooled, they'll harden a bit.

They'll be pretty fragile straight out of the oven, so let them set for a minute and then carefully transfer them to a wire rack (if you have one). Let them cool for at least 10 minutes longer. Be patient and don't touch!

Store the cookies in an airtight container for up to a week.

Honey Peppermint Cups

MAKES 12-15 PIECES

Pantry Essentials: **NATURAL SWEETENER**

I used to eat a lot of candy. I'm talking A LOT. Like, it might make you sick thinking about how much candy I used to eat. I usually went for the sticky, fruit-flavored variety—kids that were sour and bears that were gummy. But on days when I wanted chocolate, I'd go with the classic peppermint patty. I'd take it home, freeze it, and then sit down and really focus on every single bite of mintiness as I devoured it. After I changed my diet, there was no way I was going to say good-bye to my favorite chocolate treat, so I came up with a new version. These are a little richer, a lot creamier, and the best part is they only have four ingredients (and all of them you can pronounce).

2 tablespoons raw honey

¼ teaspoon peppermint extract

1 cup dairy-free chocolate or dark chocolate

Sea salt

In a small bowl, stir together the honey and peppermint until combined. Arrange mini cupcake liners on a large plate or fill a mini cupcake pan with the liners if you have one.

Melt the chocolate (if you need help with this, I have instructions on how to do it on page 170). Fill the bottom of each cup with 1 teaspoon of the melted chocolate. Add a small dollop of the honey mixture, then top it with another teaspoon of chocolate. Sprinkle a little sea salt on top of each cup. Freeze the candies for an hour and keep them frozen until ready to serve.

KITCHEN NOTES: Swap out the peppermint for rose, almond, anise, or really any oil or extract that you want to pair with chocolate.

Chocolate Mint Coin Cookies

MAKES 15–25 COOKIES

Pantry Essentials: **GRAINS, COCONUT, NATURAL SWEETENER**

The base of these cookies was inspired by a pie crust made by my friend Ashlae Warner (of Oh, Ladycakes). Before she came on my podcast, I wanted to test out one of her many amazing recipes. I decided to adapt her pie crust into little cookies. Only problem was, I didn't have any cookie cutters (as you know, I like to keep the kitchen gadgets to a minimum). But I did have a shot glass! The top of a shot glass made the perfect little circles for these cookies. I have yet to find a cookie cutter I like better. If you're fully stocked with awesome cutters, by all means, use them here. Just try to make sure whatever you use is not bigger than an inch or so wide.

1 cup pecans

1 cup thick rolled oats

¼ teaspoon sea salt

3 tablespoons coconut oil, melted

2 tablespoons real maple syrup

4½ ounces dark chocolate (or 1½ 3-ounce dark chocolate bars)

2 teaspoons peppermint extract

Preheat the oven to 325 degrees. In a food processor with the S blade attached, pulse the pecans, rolled oats, and sea salt into a fine meal texture. Drizzle in the coconut oil and maple syrup while the motor is still running until the meal begins to form a crumbly, almost wet dough.

Grab two pieces of parchment paper; line a baking sheet with one and use the other as your work surface. Press the dough mixture flat (about ⅛ or ¼ inch thick) onto your parchment paper.

Using the top of a shot glass or cookie cutter, cut out the circles. Gently slide the blade of a knife or an offset spatula under the cookie and transfer it to the baking sheet. Repeat until you have no more dough left. Bake for 7 to 10 minutes or until the cookies are slightly browned. LET COOL—as in, don't touch these or they will fall apart.

While the cookies are cooling, melt the chocolate (see page 170), then stir in the peppermint extract.

Spoon a little melted chocolate on top of each cookie and spread it into an even layer with the back of the spoon or offset spatula. Transfer the cookies, still on the baking sheet, to the fridge or freezer and cool until the chocolate has hardened. Store the cookies refrigerated in an airtight container for a week or two.

KITCHEN NOTES: This is a great cookie base recipe, so feel free to mix it up! Ditch the mint, keep the chocolate, and add nuts or seeds or a dusting of ancho chili powder to the top. Or skip the chocolate altogether and use your favorite jam or fruit topping.

Double Chocolate Cupcakes with Salted Chia Pudding Frosting

MAKES 12 CUPCAKES

Pantry Essentials: **CHIA, COCONUT, GLUTEN-FREE FLOUR, PLANT-BASED MILK, NATURAL SWEETENER**

These cupcakes remind me of that old song lyric "Make new friends, but keep the old." I've got my old friend cake and my new pal chia pudding. I like them both, and I thought it was time to bring them together. I personally love salted coconut frosting and could stand to make this one even saltier. Play around with the salt to suit your buds, just make sure to get it right before you let the pudding set in the fridge, as it will be hard to stir it after that.

FOR THE FROSTING:

1 (14-ounce) can full-fat coconut milk

5 Medjool dates, pitted and chopped

¼–½ teaspoon of sea salt

5 tablespoons chia seeds

FOR THE CUPCAKES:

1 cup unsweetened almond milk

1 tablespoon apple cider vinegar

1 tablespoon flax meal

3 tablespoons water

1 cup chickpea (garbanzo bean) flour

½ cup brown rice flour

¼ cup cocoa powder

1 teaspoon aluminum-free baking powder

½ teaspoon baking soda

½ teaspoon sea salt

2 teaspoons vanilla extract

¼ cup real maple syrup

¼ cup coconut oil, melted

1 cup dairy-free chocolate chips (I like Enjoy Life), plus more for garnish

Make the frosting: Combine the coconut milk, dates, and salt in a blender and blend until the mixture is smooth. This might take a few minutes. If you end up with small bits of dates, that's OK. But you don't want to see chunks or even white slivers of the coconut milk. The color should be a very light tan. Taste, and if you want to add more salt, do it now and then blend for a few more seconds (I really like the saltiness ½ teaspoon brings). Pour the mixture into a medium jar or container with a lid. Stir in the chia seeds. Put the frosting in the fridge, covered, for at least 6 hours (overnight is best).

For the cupcakes: Preheat the oven to 350 degrees. Line a standard cupcake pan with 12 paper liners.

In a small bowl, combine the almond milk and apple cider vinegar. In another small bowl, make a flax egg: mix the flax meal and water together. Let both the almond milk mixture and the flax egg rest for at least 10 minutes.

In a large bowl, whisk together the flours, cocoa powder, baking powder, baking soda, and salt.

Combine the vanilla, maple syrup, flax egg, and almond milk mixture in a bowl. Add the wet ingredients into the dry and stir to combine. Do not overstir. Pour in the coconut oil and chocolate chips and give it a few more stirs, until just combined.

Fill each cupcake liner with ¼ cup of the batter. Bake for 18 to 20 minutes or until a fork or toothpick inserted in the center comes out clean.

Let your cupcakes cool on a wire rack if you have one. When they're completely cool, top them with the frosting. Sprinkle a few more chocolate chips on top.

KITCHEN NOTES: Because this frosting must be refrigerated, these are a little tricky to store and are best eaten freshly made. If you're taking them to a party, I suggest adding the frosting right before you head out or, even better, when you arrive. If these are just for you at home, keep the frosting refrigerated until you're ready for a cupcake and then add it.

Chocolate Hazelnut Crispies

MAKES 15 NUT BALLS

Pantry Essentials: **NUTS, NATURAL SWEETENER, COCONUT**

When I first learned how to make crispy nut butter balls, I made them for so many parties that I had to ask a friend if it was getting weird. But she assured me that they were a hit and I should never stop making them. So here we are. I typically use store-bought almond butter for these, but wanted to take them up a notch here by using homemade nut butter and adding a Nutella-ish vibe. The coconut is optional, and I just use it because I think they look prettier this way.

1½ cups raw hazelnuts (a.k.a. filberts)

¼ cup real maple syrup

1 teaspoon vanilla extract

Tiny pinch of sea salt

2 cups gluten-free crisp rice cereal
(I like brown rice crisps best)

1 cup dairy-free or dark chocolate chips

Unsweetened coconut flakes (optional)

KITCHEN NOTES: If you don't want to make your own nut butter, by all means, buy it! You'll need to use 1 cup of it. Almond butter works great if you can't find hazelnut. If the nut butter is already salted, skip the pinch of salt.

Preheat the oven to 350 degrees and toast the hazelnuts on a baking sheet until they are dark and fragrant, 10 to 15 minutes. Let them cool. Remove their skins by placing them in between two paper towels and rubbing back and forth. Important: This does not have to be perfect. You might not be able to remove all the skins, and that's totally cool. Move on and don't drive yourself crazy.

In a food processor with the S blade attached, process the hazelnuts until you form a smooth nut butter. This could take up to 5 minutes. Be patient. While you're blending, grab a big plate or baking sheet and line it with parchment paper.

In a large bowl, combine the hazelnut butter, maple syrup, vanilla, and salt. Stir in the rice crisps.

Roll the mixture into a ball a little smaller than a Ping-Pong ball. Place the balls on the parchment-covered plate or baking sheet.

Melt the chocolate (see page 170).

Drizzle melted chocolate over each ball. Add a sprinkle of coconut for some added prettiness. Freeze the balls until you're ready to serve. These taste best frozen or slightly frozen.

Nut Butter Chocolate Tart

MAKES 8 SERVINGS

Pantry Essentials: **NUT BUTTER, NATURAL SWEETENER, COCONUT**

One bite of this rich and creamy tart, and you'll think maybe this whole plant-based thing isn't so bad. It's an all-season tart—nut butter and coconut are always available—making it the perfect dessert to bring to parties all year long.

1 cup almond meal

¼ teaspoon sea salt

1 cup rolled oats

1 teaspoon vanilla extract

3 tablespoons real maple syrup

1 tablespoon coconut oil, melted

1 cup dark or dairy-free chocolate chips, roughly chopped

2 (14-ounce) cans full-fat coconut milk, refrigerated overnight

¾ cup natural nut butter

4 Medjool dates (the stickier the better), pits removed, diced

Pinch of sea salt, if needed

Preheat the oven to 350 degrees. Grease a 9-inch tart pan. If you don't have a tart pan, that's OK. Use a pie pan. The crust won't come up all the way to the top of the pan, so just bring it as high as you can and press it against the sides of the pan (make sure they are well greased).

In a food processor with the S blade attached, pulse the almond meal, salt, and oats together. While the motor is running, pour in the vanilla, maple syrup, and coconut oil. Blend until you don't see whole oats anymore and you have a nice crumbly dough ball.

Press the dough into the prepared pan and bake the crust for 10 to 12 minutes or until the edges and bottom begin to brown.

As soon as you remove the pan from the oven, use the back of a spoon to press down any of the dough that has bubbled up, then immediately sprinkle ½ cup of the chocolate pieces on the bottom of the crust. Make sure to evenly distribute the chocolate chips. Do not let the crust cool before doing this—act fast! When the chocolate becomes shiny and is melting onto the crust, use a knife or a small spatula to smooth it over the bottom of the crust.

Make the coconut cream, following the instructions on page 170. In your food processor, process your nut butter and dates until combined; if you use unsalted nut butter, add the salt. Add the nut butter mixture to the coconut cream and mix until combined. Taste and add more salt if needed.

Pour the filling into the crust and smooth the top with the back of a spoon. Sprinkle the remaining ½ cup chocolate over the top of the pie. Chill it for at least two hours before serving.

Roasted Pineapple Sundaes

MAKES 4-6 SERVINGS

Pantry Essentials: **NATURAL SWEETENER, COCONUT**

On every episode of my podcast, I ask each guest to share a plant-based recipe they love. All of the recipes are hits, but the most memorable one came from comedian and actor Jeff Garlin. He said his favorite dessert recipe was pretty simple: get a pineapple, cut into slices. Done. As an ode to Jeff, I decided to make a pineapple dessert where the pineapple itself is the star of the show. Here I've roasted it to bring out its sweetness and added some texture with coconut, and then serve it with ice cream to create a tropical treat. Keep any leftover pineapple topping in the fridge and stir it into oatmeal or coconut yogurt.

1 pineapple, peeled, cored, and cut into 1-inch cubes

½ teaspoon cinnamon

1 tablespoon real maple syrup

⅓ cup unsweetened coconut flakes

Dairy-free vanilla ice cream

Preheat the oven to 450 degrees and line a baking sheet with parchment paper.

In a large bowl, combine the pineapple, cinnamon, and maple syrup and let the mixture sit for about 10 minutes. Remove the pineapple from the bowl with a slotted spoon so you drain most of the juice (the maple syrup and pineapple juice will burn quickly, so you don't want too much on the baking sheet as you roast the fruit).

Spread the pineapple on the prepared sheet and roast it for 15 minutes. Sprinkle the coconut flakes on the pineapple. It's OK if some of the coconut lands on the parchment. Roast for another 5 to 7 minutes. You want the coconut to toast but not burn, so make sure to watch the oven. When the coconut is slightly browned, remove the pan from the oven and let it cool slightly.

Scoop some ice cream into bowls or parfait glasses and top it with the warm pineapple. Make sure to scrape up the coconut bits that have caramelized during roasting and sprinkle them over the sundae. Serve immediately. Store the remaining pineapple in an airtight container in the fridge for a few days.

Notes from the Field: Accepting Change

It's about to get emotional for a minute. Bear with me....

About four months into overhauling my diet, I was feeling crazy-good one morning. I was lying in bed, grinning from ear to ear, thinking about how much I had changed—my body was no longer in pain, my energy level was insane, my skin looked great. I was really happy. But as I thought about all these changes, I started to feel a little sad. The old me was starting to disappear to make room for the new me. And I'm not just talking about the physical changes; I'm talking about my old identity and who I thought I was.

I used to be the friend you could pig out with. The girl who thought healthy eating and yoga were for fancy people (not me). The girl who never cooked and loved making jokes about just how undomestic she was. But I wasn't that person anymore.

It sounds crazy, but I had to mourn that old me a little. She'd been with me for my whole life but was leaving now for greener pastures (literally). I had to accept that I no longer enjoyed cheese benders—I ate cashew cream (really!?). I could go to the movies and enjoy it without a big tub of popcorn (I always thought that people who did this were aliens). And most days, I looked in the mirror and saw a completely different person. I had a new glow.

Even after five years, I'm still adjusting to this change. Sometimes I'll look at my cart in the checkout line and think it's someone else's. Or when a waiter asks if I have any dietary restrictions, I pause so long that one of my friends has to chime in and say "YES!"—to make it easier on us all.

The reality is that the person I am now is the person I'd always dreamed of being. As much as I knocked healthy people and those no-popcorn eaters, I wanted to look and feel as good as they did, and I just didn't think I had the will or dedication to do it. Maybe I didn't think I deserved it.

But now that I'm here and I know how good it feels, I never want to leave. As you begin to change your diet and add more plants, you might have to say "so long" to some of your old traditions and rituals. And that's OK. Real, whole food is powerful and can dramatically change your life. That doesn't mean that you need to forget the old you. Celebrate her and keep all the things that make her special. But you might need to let go of the things that just weren't making you feel your best.

Coconut Date Pinwheels

MAKES 14-16 SLICES

Pantry Essentials: **NUT BUTTER, COCONUT, NATURAL SWEETENER**

When the UK cooking show *The Great British Bake Off* made its television debut in the US, I watched an entire season in three days. I was obsessed. One of my favorite desserts to watch the contestants make was the classic Swiss roll. After my binge watch, I went to the kitchen to create my own version of this dessert. Now, technically, there's no cake here, but I've got the roll part nailed. I hope Mary Berry would approve.

1 cup Medjool dates, pits removed

2 tablespoons natural almond or peanut butter

Sea salt

1 cup unsweetened coconut flakes

In a food processor, process the dates, nut butter, and a pinch of salt until a ball of dough forms. Be patient; this might take a few minutes. Taste the dough and decide whether you want to add more salt. If so, add it now and process for another few seconds. Depending on the stickiness of your dates, a ball might not form all the way. That's OK. Use a spatula or spoon to scrape down the sides of the food processor, collect the dough, and make your own ball.

On a piece of parchment or wax paper, press out the dough with your hands. Do your best to spread it evenly. It should be about ⅛ inch thick and 7 or 8 inches wide. You may need to wet your hands a bit to keep it from sticking as you work. Sprinkle ½ cup of the coconut over the dough, the same way you would put cheese on a pizza. Go right to the edge.

Starting at the end facing you, carefully roll the dough as tightly as you can. If it begins to crack, pinch it back together and smooth it over with your fingers. Keep rolling until you reach the end and then smooth over the seam of the dough with your fingers. You'll have a pretty long log of dough at this point.

Spread the remaining ½ cup coconut on the parchment and roll the log back and forth into the coconut to cover it. Use your hands to press any remaining coconut into the log.

Roll the parchment paper around the log and freeze it for at least 6 hours or overnight. Store in the freezer wrapped in parchment until ready to serve. When you're ready to serve, slice it into 1-inch pieces.

KITCHEN NOTES: The ends of your pinwheel won't be pretty enough to serve. Cut them off and reserve these as your own secret stash in the freezer.

Turtle Eggs

MAKES 10-15 PIECES

Pantry Essentials: **NATURAL SWEETENER, NUTS**

I brought a couple of these turtle eggs to my friend Connor to taste test them, and here's how the conversation went:

> Connor: Yum, what's the center?
> Me: Just dates, a little salt, and a pecan.
> Connor: Cool. And caramel?
> Me: No, just dates, a little sea salt, and a pecan.
> Connor: So there's no caramel?
> Me: No.

Ten minutes later...

> Connor: So just dates? Sure there is no caramel?
> Me: OMG. I'll just send you the recipe, OK?

It really is hard to believe you can create something that tastes just like caramel by blending dates and salt, so I can't blame Connor for asking (repeatedly). The possibilities are endless when it comes to this planty caramel...but these turtles are a great place to start.

2 cups Medjool dates, pits removed

¼–½ teaspoon sea salt, plus more if needed

18 pecans (1 for each turtle, so a couple extra just in case)

1 cup dairy-free or dark chocolate pieces

Line a baking sheet with parchment or wax paper.

In a food processor, process the dates and ¼ teaspoon salt until a ball of dough forms. Be patient; this might take a few minutes. Taste the dough, and if you want to add more salt, add it now and process for another few seconds. Depending on the stickiness of your dates, a ball might not form all the way. That's OK. Use a spatula or spoon to scrape down the sides of the food processor, collect the dough, and make your own ball.

Roll the dough into heaping teaspoon-size balls. Press a pecan into the center of each and pinch the dough around it to seal the pecan in there. Form the ball into an egg shape. You may need to wet your hands while doing this; it can get a little sticky.

Transfer the eggs to the prepared baking sheet and put them in the freezer for an hour.

While the dough freezes, melt the chocolate (see page 170).

Drop each turtle into the chocolate to coat it fully, then scoop it out with a fork, shaking it a little so the extra chocolate falls through the tines. Transfer the chocolate-coated eggs back to the prepared baking sheet and sprinkle each one with a little sea salt if you like. Return them to the freezer until the chocolate has set and you are ready to serve.

KITCHEN NOTE: Sticky dates are going to work best for this recipe. If your dates are fairly dry and not sticky, soak them in hot water for about 10 minutes, then drain them well before using them.

Chocolate Chunk Cookies

MAKES 20 COOKIES

Pantry Essentials: **GLUTEN-FREE FLOUR, COCONUT, NATURAL SWEETENER**

This is the dessert that I like to serve to plant-based-eating skeptics. No one can ever believe these cookies are all the "frees" (gluten, dairy, refined-sugar, and soy). They are super rich and buttery, just like the cookies most of us grew up with (you know the ones whose recipe came from the back of the chocolate chip bag). Before I take all the credit, I want to give major props to my friend Jamie Stelter (of *TV Dinner* and NY1 fame) for inspiring this recipe. She created the base for these cookies and challenged me to make them 100 percent OPP.

1 tablespoon flax meal

3 tablespoons water

2 cups almond meal

½ cup brown rice flour

1 teaspoon sea salt

1 teaspoon baking soda

½ cup pure maple syrup

2 teaspoons vanilla extract

⅓ cup coconut oil, melted

1 cup dairy-free chocolate chunks or dark chocolate

KITCHEN NOTES: In the summer, I like making these a tiny bit smaller and making them into ice cream sandwiches with coconut or cashew ice cream.

Preheat the oven to 375 degrees and line a baking sheet with parchment paper. Make a flax egg: mix the flax meal and water in a small bowl or glass and set it aside for at least 10 minutes.

Whisk together the flours, salt, and baking soda in a medium-size bowl. Combine the maple syrup, vanilla, and flax egg in a large bowl. Begin to pour the flour mix into the bowl of liquids a little at a time, stirring as you go. When it is all incorporated, pour in the coconut oil and chocolate chips and give it a few more stirs.

Use a tablespoon to drop the dough onto the prepared sheet. These cookies won't spread much, so you can put them pretty close together. Bake the cookies for 10 minutes, then check on them. They should be slightly brown on top and still feel a little bit doughy. If they're not there yet, you can bake them for a minute or two longer, but you don't want to overcook these. After they've cooled, they'll harden a bit. Store them refrigerated in an airtight container for up to one week or in the freezer for even longer (I like cold cookies).

Triple Berry Skillet Cobbler

MAKES 6 SERVINGS

Pantry Essentials: **GLUTEN-FREE FLOUR, PLANT-BASED MILK, NATURAL SWEETENER**

I once had a piece of olive oil cake that I still dream about. I remember exactly how it tasted—it wasn't too sweet, yet it was such a perfect dessert. When I changed my diet, I became a coconut-oil-or-bust kind of woman—it just works so well as a butter substitute for baking. But the other day, that olive oil cake popped into my head again and I wanted to see if I could incorporate olive oil into my baking. I decided to swap out the coconut oil I typically use to make this cobbler and use a little olive oil instead...and it worked!

This cobbler definitely tastes best the day it's made. So, if you're planning on serving this to guests, take that into account. Dream scenario, I'd throw this in the oven as people sit down to the table and serve it warm after dinner.

1 tablespoon minced mint leaves

Zest of 1 small lime

4 cups berries of your choice
(I like blueberries, blackberries, and strawberries—if you use strawberries and blackberries, make sure to slice or chop them)

½ cup plus 2 tablespoons real maple syrup

1 cup almond meal

½ cup brown rice flour

1½ teaspoons aluminum-free baking powder

1 teaspoon sea salt

¾ cup almond milk

1 teaspoon vanilla extract

2 tablespoons good olive oil

Coconut cream or dairy-free ice cream

KITCHEN NOTES: If you want to make this cobbler when berries aren't in season, use frozen ones—just make sure to thaw the berries all the way and thoroughly strain out their juice. The extra juice will make this cobbler soggy in the middle.

Preheat the oven to 350 degrees.

Combine the mint, lime, berries, and 2 tablespoons of maple syrup in a medium bowl.

Grease a 10-inch cast-iron skillet with a generous amount of olive oil and place it in the oven for at least 5 minutes.

While the skillet is heating up, make the batter. Combine the flours, baking powder, and salt in a large bowl. Pour in the almond milk, the remaining ½ cup maple syrup, and vanilla and stir until just combined. Do not overstir. Stir in the olive oil last.

Pour the batter into the hot skillet. Top it with the berry mixture. Make sure to bring the berries all the way to the edge of the batter. Bake until the cobbler has browned around the edges and the center is cooked through, 50 to 55 minutes. Let the cobbler cool slightly and cut it into slices. Serve it topped with coconut cream or ice cream.

No-Bake Tahini Cherry Bars

MAKES 8 BARS

Pantry Essentials: **TAHINI, COCONUT, NATURAL SWEETENER**

Sharing homemade desserts with my friends and family is one of my favorite things to do. I love making cobblers and big batches of cookies to bring to parties or drop off at people's homes. But when it comes to these bars—they're just for me. It's not that I'm being greedy, it's that these bars aren't the best travelers. Similar to ice cream, out of the freezer, they don't hold together very well. But who says you have to share every dessert? I always like to have a stash of these in the freezer just for my family and me (mainly me). They're super easy to make and are the perfect combination of tart and sweet. I love using dried cherries, but you could easily sub in dried cranberries, too.

2 tablespoons coconut oil

1 teaspoon vanilla extract

3 tablespoons real maple syrup

⅓ cup tahini

Small pinch of sea salt

1¼ cups rolled oats

¼ cup unsweetened dried cherries
(if they are large, cut them in half)

Line a 4-by-8-inch loaf pan with parchment paper.

On low heat, melt the coconut oil in a medium-size saucepan. Remove it from the heat and immediately stir in the vanilla and maple syrup. Stir in the tahini and salt. Add the oats and stir until they are fully coated with tahini mixture. Stir in the cherries.

Press the dough into the loaf pan. It might seem a little crumbly, and you might think you did something wrong, but you didn't. Just keep pressing. Once it freezes, it will bind together.

Freeze the dough for at least 45 minutes. Cut it into bars and eat it immediately. Store leftovers covered in the freezer until you've eaten them all.

Julia Turshen's Strawberry Granita with Whipped Coconut Cream

MAKES 4 SERVINGS

Pantry Essentials: **COCONUT, NATURAL SWEETENER**

Julia Turshen is just plain cool. Her vibe, her food, her writing, even her hair…it's hard to think of a better word to describe her than *cool*. When I asked my podcast listeners what chefs they wanted to see in my book, she was at the top of their list (and mine too), so I'm really stoked that she agreed to share a recipe here.

If you're not familiar with Julia's work, she's coauthored a bunch of cookbooks with lots of famous faces. But her solo mission as an author, *Small Victories,* is my favorite. She loves clean and simple recipes that are still super delicious, and this one has got those qualities. Plus, she made it, so it's automatically…cool.

1 pint (about 2 cups) strawberries, hulled and sliced

2 tablespoons fresh lemon juice

2 teaspoons coconut sugar

2 teaspoons vanilla extract

Kosher salt

1 (14-ounce) can full-fat coconut milk, chilled

WHAT JULIA SAYS ABOUT THIS RECIPE:

When my wife, Grace, was diagnosed with diabetes, I immediately set to work to figure out what treats she could eat that satisfied her sweet tooth without increasing her blood sugar levels. This combination of a bright strawberry granita and decadent coconut cream not only fulfills all of our new dietary requirements, it's also totally delicious.

Place the strawberries, lemon juice, coconut sugar, 1 teaspoon of the vanilla, and a pinch of salt in a high-speed blender and whiz until the mixture is smooth. Transfer it to a shallow container and freeze until it's solid, about 2 hours.

When you're ready to serve, open the chilled can of coconut milk, being careful not to shake it (you don't want the coconut water and coconut fat to combine), and scoop the hard, thickened cream into a bowl. Reserve the liquid for another use such as smoothies. Add the remaining 1 teaspoon vanilla and pinch of salt to the coconut cream and whip with a whisk or a handheld electric mixer until it is thick and creamy, about 1 minute.

Scrape the strawberry mixture with the tines of a fork to form flakes. Divide the whipped coconut cream and strawberry granita among four glasses, alternating them to form layers. Serve immediately!

Roasted Berry Milkshake

MAKES 2 SERVINGS

Pantry Essentials: **NATURAL SWEETENER, PLANT-BASED MILK**

Dairy-free ice cream has come a long way over the last few years. I remember going to the grocery store not so long ago and finding only one or two brands. They didn't really didn't taste that great and always seemed to have freezer burn. Now there are dozens of options! At my local store, I can find ice cream made with cashew, almond, and coconut milk—and many of them taste even better than the "real" thing. I used cashew cream for this milkshake, because it's a bit creamier than other nut milks—but coconut or almond would work well, too.

1 cup fresh blackberries

1 cup fresh blueberries

1 tablespoon real maple syrup

1 tablespoon fresh lemon juice

¼ cup unsweetened almond milk,
plus more if needed

2 cups nondairy ice cream (I like cashew)

KITCHEN NOTES: You can take this up a notch and roast the berries with some real vanilla. Just open a vanilla bean and scrape the seeds into the berries along with the maple syrup. Use your hands or a spoon to distribute the seeds evenly; the vanilla can get a little clumpy.

Preheat the oven to 400 degrees. Line a deep baking dish with parchment paper. Set aside a few of the berries to use for garnish, then dump the rest into the dish and toss them with the maple syrup and lemon juice. Roast the berries for 15 to 20 minutes, until they start to release their juices. Let them cool completely.

Transfer the berries and their juices from roasting to a high-speed blender with the almond milk. Blend on low to mix the berries and milk, but not enough to break up the berries completely. Add the ice cream and blend on medium speed just until combined. Do not overblend. If you do, the ice cream will melt and you won't get the thick milkshake consistency. If it's too thick, add a little more almond milk before serving. Serve with the reserved berries on top.

Grasshopper Parfait

MAKES 4-5 SERVINGS

Pantry Essentials: **NUTS, COCONUT, NATURAL SWEETENER**

This is a little riff on one of my all-time favorite desserts, grasshopper pie. I'm all about it, except for one thing: the cream is usually dyed with green food coloring to appear more "minty." Food coloring is made up of a few ingredients—water, petroleum, synthetic chemicals, and more synthetic chemicals. These are chemicals that are actually banned in other countries but have not been regulated here in the US.

For this reason, I generally steer clear of food coloring. But I really wanted to keep the classic green cream for this dessert, so I looked around my fridge and saw my little bottle of liquid chlorophyll! I realize that this is not an ingredient that everyone has on hand, so it's optional. If you do decide to add it, a little goes a long way, so start with just a drop or two and go from there. You can use it down the road for holiday cookies and egg dyeing, too.

1 cup raw pecans

½ cup rolled oats

¼ cup cocoa powder

½ teaspoon sea salt

¼ cup plus 2 tablespoons real maple syrup

2 tablespoons coconut oil, melted

1 cup dairy-free chocolate or dark chocolate chips

1 (14-ounce) can full-fat coconut milk, refrigerated overnight

1–1½ teaspoons peppermint extract or flavoring

1–3 drops liquid chlorophyll (optional)

Preheat the oven to 350 degrees and line a 9-inch square pan with parchment paper.

In a food processor with the S blade attached, process the pecans, oats, cocoa, and salt for about 30 seconds, until a meal starts to form. Drizzle in ¼ cup of the maple syrup and the coconut oil while the motor is still running and process until the meal begins to form a dough ball. Scrape down the sides of the processer and transfer the dough ball to the prepared pan.

Press the dough evenly into the pan. It can be sticky, so you may need to wet your fingertips a little bit. Once the dough is pressed in, cover it with the chocolate chips. Press the chips into the dough. They won't be covered by the dough; they just need to be pressed into the top.

Bake the dough for 12 to 15 minutes, until it's cooked through but has a nice bounce to it. Don't overbake—you want the texture to still be a little soft. Let it cool.

Follow the instructions on page 170 to whip the coconut cream until it is light and fluffy. Add the mint and the remaining 2 tablespoons maple syrup to the coconut cream and blend again until they're incorporated.

If you want to use the chlorophyll, start with a drop and blend again (a little goes a long way). Add more until you get the color you want.

Carefully lift the cooled cookie out of the pan by holding two sides of the parchment paper. Cut it into ½- to 1-inch square cookie pieces.

In individual shallow bowls or glasses (I love to use stemless wine glasses for this), add a layer of cookies. Add a couple tablespoons of coconut cream, then layer the other half of the cookies on top and add a little more cream. Serve right away!

KITCHEN NOTES: If you decide to buy liquid chlorophyll, you can find it in the vitamin section of most health food and some grocery stores. I like getting the kind that has a mint flavor; chlorophyll can taste pretty intense without it. After you use it for this recipe, you can add a few drops to your water each day. I wouldn't suggest dropping it straight into your mouth without the water. It's so concentrated that you'll have green teeth for most of the day!

TASTERS TELL ALL…

"I am NOT a chocolate person or a 'sweets' person, and was worried this would be too sweet and chocolaty for my liking. Boy, was I wrong. I'm so in love with the combo of flavors and textures and, most of all, how I literally made it in less time than it takes me to find a parking spot at Trader Joe's."

Crispy Ice Cream Bars

MAKES 16 BARS

Pantry Essentials: **NATURAL SWEETENER, NUT BUTTER**

This banana ice cream is unbelievably creamy and unbelievably dairy-free. After you taste it, you might decide to just eat it straight up and not even finish making this recipe. If you can resist the temptation, however, keep in mind that the ice cream gets pretty hard when it freezes—so be sure to let the bars thaw for a bit before cutting them and diving in. I love adding extra mix-ins for these bars—chocolate chunks, cacao nibs, or nut pieces are all great options. Stir in your favorites after you make the ice cream and before you freeze it.

3 cups crisp brown rice cereal (not puffed)

1 tablespoon cinnamon

3 tablespoons real maple syrup

5 bananas, peeled, cut into 1-inch coins, and frozen overnight

1 cup plus 1 tablespoon crunchy natural nut butter (I used almond)

1 tablespoon raw honey, plus extra for serving

1 tablespoon coconut oil

Generous pinch of sea salt

Mix-in options: chocolate chunks, cacao nibs, walnuts, pecan pieces

Preheat the oven to 350 degrees and line a baking sheet with parchment paper. Also line an 8-inch square metal pan with a slightly oversize piece of parchment paper, so the paper hangs over the sides of the pan.

In a medium bowl, combine the cereal and cinnamon. Add the maple syrup. With your hands, toss the ingredients together for a minute to coat the crisps well. Spread them on the prepared baking sheet and bake them for 5 minutes. Set them aside to cool.

Meanwhile, let the bananas thaw for about 10 minutes, then put them in a food processor and pulse the frozen pieces for about 30 seconds to break them up a bit. Add the nut butter, honey, coconut oil, and salt and process until you have a smooth frozen-yogurt-like consistency. You may need to stop the food processor from time to time to loosen up stuck bananas. If you want mix-ins, use a spoon to incorporate them now.

Break up any of the crisps that may have stuck together during baking and line the bottom of the

square pan with half of the crisps. Pour the ice cream mixture on top of the crisp layer and use the back of a spoon or spatula to spread it evenly. Top the ice cream layer with the remaining crisps.

Cover the pan and freeze it for at least 6 hours or overnight.

When you're ready to eat, remove the pan from the freezer and let it sit for about 5 minutes. Cut it into 16 slices and drizzle them with honey before serving.

9 | Snacks + Sips

GRILLED CINNAMON AND BANANA SANDWICH

CURRY CORN

BEET AND APPLE SAUCE

SWEET AND SPICY NUTS

TAHINI BALL BALLS

PEACH GINGER TEA

PISTACHIO COCONUT SQUARES

STRAWBERRY BASIL COOLER

WATERMELON LEMONADE

THREE SIMPLE JUICE RECIPES
(CARROT AND ORANGE, GREEN APPLE, GREEN DREAM)

CHOCOLATE MILK/HOT CHOCOLATE

Grilled Cinnamon and Banana Sandwich

MAKES 1 SERVING

Pantry Essentials: **NUT BUTTER, COCONUT**

I debated the serving size for this recipe. I could have doubled or tripled it to serve more, but there's something about this warm and comforting sandwich that feels like a solo mission. If you don't like bananas (hi, Mom), use some strawberries instead. And I highly suggest eating it in your pajamas.

1 tablespoon natural nut butter (I like almond)

¼ teaspoon cinnamon

2 teaspoons coconut oil

2 slices whole grain, sprouted, or gluten-free bread

½ banana, peeled and cut into ½ inch coins

In a small bowl, combine the nut butter and cinnamon (feel free to use some extra nut butter for a richer sandwich).

Spread coconut oil on one side of each slice of bread. Spread nut butter on the opposite of each side.

In a skillet, on medium-high, place one slice of bread nut butter side up and arrange the bananas on top. Cover it with the other slice of bread, nut butter side down.

Grill each side for 3 to 5 minutes or until the bread becomes brown and crispy. Eat immediately.

Curry Corn

Pantry Essential: **GLUTEN-FREE GRAINS**

Before I changed my diet, when my endometriosis was at its worst, I stayed in most weekend nights. And most of those nights were spent in bed. My husband always tried to cheer me up by offering to join me and have a movie and popcorn night in bed. This curry corn is the popcorn we would make every time. The recipe seems super simple, but there's something about the way the curry powder and salt come together that makes this popcorn special. We still have lots of movie-and-popcorn nights in bed, but now it's not because I have to stay in...it's when I want to.

½ cup organic popcorn kernels

3 tablespoons olive oil

1 teaspoon curry powder

1 teaspoon sea salt

Add the kernels and 2 tablespoons of the oil to a pot, turn the heat to high, and cover. As the kernels start to pop, continually shake the pan to keep them from sticking. As popping slows, turn off the heat and wait for the popping to stop. Stir in the remaining oil, tossing to make sure it gets distributed evenly. Sprinkle in curry powder and salt and stir again. Serve.

Notes from the Field:
Shine Blockers and How to Deal with People Who Aren't Down with Your Plant Eating

———

shine blocker (noun):
a person who blocks your shine

When I first started making changes to my diet, there were people in my life who weren't completely down with my new way of eating. They fell into two categories.

Category One: People who thought I was being weird/new age/extreme. These people didn't say much, just gave an exaggerated "really?" or a quizzical side-eye when I mentioned the term *plant-based*. You have to remember, I had never cooked before, let alone cooked vegetables. I understood their skepticism. This group was pretty harmless, because I could feel their love as they witnessed the positive changes taking place in my life.

Category Two: People who were secretly annoyed and upset that I was doing something that would interfere with our food relationship. No more pizza nights together. No more cookie swaps. These were the worst offenders and biggest shine blockers, because their negativity was subtle—little digs that made me question whether I was doing the right thing.

Food is a tricky thing. There is so much tradition and emotion tied to it. We use it to celebrate, to mourn, to connect with family and friends. When people feel like you are threatening these traditions and connections, all sorts of emotions can come to the surface.

Instead of giving them the slow fade-out of my life, I decided to fade them in. I made an effort to include them in my new food world—having a smoothie date, baking them plant-based cookies, and still going to our favorite restaurants, but ordering a little differently than before. And it started to work. I noticed a shift in their attitude, and it was because they felt included. I also think they realized that my new food didn't taste as bad as they thought it would.

I'm happy to report that the Category One offenders are now mostly onboard. The Category Twos are a mixed bag. Some aren't as close to me anymore, while others are closer than they've ever been. Remember that you are making the decision to eat more real food because you want to feel good. This is about YOU—no one else. Don't let other people's negativity stop you from feeling your best.

Beet and Apple Sauce

MAKES 4 ADULT-SIZE OR 10 KID-SIZE SERVINGS

Pantry Essential: **NATURAL SWEETENER**

Every time I go to my in-laws' house, I leave with bags full of groceries. My husband's mom, Reen, loves buying us odds and ends from the store—a roll of a thousand trash bags here, a tub of cashews there. It's always great stuff. On one occasion, she sent me off with ten packs of cooked beets (there were four in a pack!). It was more beets than our fridge could hold, so I came up with this recipe to use up some of them. It's great for grown-ups, but also pretty ideal for little ones as they start to eat solid foods.

3 small apples, peeled and quartered

3 medium beets, cooked and peeled (see page 85 or use precooked beets)

1 cinnamon stick

½ cup water

2 tablespoons orange juice or lemon juice

Real maple syrup

In a small pot, combine the apples, beets, cinnamon stick, and water. Cover the pot, bring it to a simmer, and cook for about 10 minutes or until the apples are soft and begin to fall apart.

Remove the cinnamon stick and transfer the mixture to a high-speed blender. Blend until you reach whatever consistency you want. You can keep it chunky or go super smooth. Transfer the sauce to your storage jar and stir in the orange juice. Let it cool a bit before you add the maple syrup. Start with 1 teaspoon and then taste. Depending on how sweet your apples are, you may or may not want to add more. Store the sauce refrigerated in an airtight container for up to a week.

Serve it as is or with a handful of granola for some added crunch.

Sweet and Spicy Nuts

MAKES 2 CUPS

Pantry Essentials: **NUTS, NATURAL SWEETENER, COCONUT**

As neat as I try to keep my cupboards, there always seem to be a dozen little crumpled bags from the bulk section, each with a handful of nuts inside. None of the bags actually have enough to make a proper recipe, but I really don't like wasting food...so I keep them all. I know I'll use them eventually. This recipe is that perfect "eventually." I round up all the scraps of nuts and then bake them with some spices and coconut. These nuts are really great for parties, road trips, and sneaking into the movie theater for a snack.

2 cups raw nuts, shells removed
(a mix of whatever you have—pistachios, almonds, cashews, walnuts, pecans)

3 tablespoons real maple syrup

2 teaspoons olive oil or melted coconut oil

1 teaspoon cinnamon

Pinch of cayenne

Pinch of sea salt

Handful of unsweetened coconut flakes or shreds

Preheat the oven to 350 degrees and line a baking sheet with parchment paper.

In a large bowl, combine all the ingredients. Toss the nuts to make sure they are thoroughly coated with your spices. Transfer them to the prepared baking sheet, being careful to spread them out, and bake for 10 to 15 minutes, flipping them with a spatula halfway through. Watch the nuts to make sure they don't burn. Let them cool and serve. They will keep in a sealed container for a few weeks.

Tahini Ball Balls

MAKES 10-12 PIECES

Pantry Essentials: **TAHINI, COCONUT, GRAINS, NATURAL SWEETENER**

My son's favorite snack is these little things he calls "ball balls." The original version was made of nut butter blended with some dates and coconut and then rolled into a ball. It was a lunchtime staple for us, but when he started going to school, there were strict guidelines about his classroom being a nut-free zone. No more ball balls?! No way. I swapped out the nut butter for tahini and added a little honey. This version is safe for all the kids in his class. Ball balls are back!

¼ cup tahini

¼ cup rolled oats or hemp seeds

¼ cup unsweetened coconut flakes or shreds

2 teaspoons raw honey or real maple syrup

2 Medjool dates (the stickier the better), pitted

Sea salt

In a food processor with the S blade attached, process all the ingredients together. You will have a pretty crumbly dough that doesn't look like it will form balls, but it will. Take bite-size pieces and roll them in the palms of your hands. If the dough is too sticky, wet your hands a little bit. Refrigerate them for about 30 minutes before eating. Store them in the fridge until they're gone.

TASTERS TELL ALL...

"I added cacao nibs to these. It was delish and added a little bitterness that really complemented the sweetness of the coconut, honey, and dates. I would also try rolling the balls in cacao powder. F yes!"

Peach Ginger Tea

MAKES 2 SERVINGS

Pantry Essentials: **NATURAL SWEETENER**

Until recently, I wasn't into tea. In college, I would order it to look cool, but it pretty much just kept my hands warm. As soon I began to change my diet and my taste buds followed suit, I suddenly became a "tea person." Hardcore/purist tea drinkers would say this recipe is blasphemy and tea shall not be mixed with fruit. I get it. But why not mix it up every now and then and be whatever kind of tea person you want to be? You can add any frozen fruit here or a combination of a few.

**2 cups brewed green tea,
cooled to room temperature**

1 cup frozen peaches

Thumb-size knob of fresh ginger, peeled

1–2 teaspoons raw honey (optional)

Combine the tea, peaches, and ginger in a high-speed blender and blend until the mixture is smooth and slightly frothy. Taste and add honey if you want it sweeter, then blend again. Pour into glasses and serve.

Pistachio Coconut Squares

MAKES 12 SQUARES

Pantry Essentials: **NUTS, NATURAL SWEETENER, GLUTEN-FREE GRAINS**

I wasn't quite sure how to categorize these little squares for this book. I decided they weren't sweet enough to be a dessert. A breakfast food? Not really. But after I made a big batch of them, I kept reaching for them when I was looking for something "snacky." Especially after a workout. So I trusted my tummy on this one, and they landed here in the snack chapter. With that said, make a batch and see what your tummy thinks. Eat them whatever time of day you please.

1 cup raw shelled pistachios

1 cup rolled oats

½ teaspoon sea salt

¼ cup real maple syrup

2 tablespoons olive oil

⅓ cup unsweetened coconut flakes

Raw honey (optional)

Preheat the oven to 350 degrees and line a 9-inch square pan with parchment paper.

In a food processor with the S blade attached, process the pistachios, oats, and salt for about 30 seconds, until a meal starts to form. Drizzle in the maple syrup and olive oil while the motor is still running until the meal begins to come together into a crumbly, almost-wet dough.

Press the dough evenly into the pan and cover it with coconut flakes. Bake for 10 to 12 minutes, until the coconut is nice and golden brown and the dough is cooked through. You want the squares to still be a little soft—don't overbake these.

Carefully lift the cooled dough out of the pan by holding two sides of the parchment paper. Cut it into squares. Drizzle a little honey over the top for extra sweetness, if you like. Store the squares in a sealed container for up to a week.

KITCHEN NOTES: You can rough-chop a handful of pistachios and mix them in with the coconut topping for extra crunch and color.

Strawberry Basil Cooler

MAKES 2 SERVINGS

Pantry Essential: **COCONUT**

This is the perfect summertime/it's-January-and-I-wish-it-were-summertime drink. Because the recipe calls for frozen strawberries, you don't have to wait until berries are in season (i.e., aren't six dollars a pint) to make it. After you've tried this one out, experiment with different frozen fruits and fresh herb combos—blackberry and mint or pineapple and cilantro come to mind. Tequila comes to mind, too....This would be a great base for a cocktail.

2 cups unsweetened coconut water

1 cup frozen strawberries

3–5 fresh basil leaves

1 tablespoon real maple syrup or raw honey (optional)

2 lime wedges

Put the coconut water, strawberries, and basil in a high-speed blender and blend on high until the mixture is smooth. Depending on how sweet your berries are, you might want some extra sweetener, so taste and add a little maple syrup or honey if needed, then blend again. Pour it into glasses, give each a squeeze of lime, and drink up.

NEXT LEVEL: After you've poured this into the glasses, add a scoop of chia seeds to each serving and stir. Let it sit for a few minutes to allow the chia to expand and then drink.

Watermelon Lemonade

MAKES 4 SERVINGS

Pantry Essential: **NATURAL SWEETENER**

Traditional lemonades are made with white sugar, water, and lemons. A lot of sugar. I get it—it's usually the reason lemonade tastes so good. I didn't take out the sweetener for this lemonade, I just made it more natural by combining maple syrup with a homemade watermelon syrup to replace the white sugar. One warning about this recipe: I really love tart lemonade. If it's a little too much for you, add more maple syrup and water to adjust for your taste buds. Also remember that pouring it over ice always takes the pucker down a notch.

4 cups watermelon cubes, seeds removed

¼ cup real maple syrup

3½ cups water

1 cup fresh lemon juice (5 or 6 lemons)

Mint leaves (optional)

Blend the watermelon cubes in a high-speed blender until smooth. Strain the mixture through a sieve into a small pot. (If you have a juicer, you can skip the blending and sieve steps and use that instead.)

Transfer the watermelon juice to a small saucepan and add the maple syrup, Simmer over low for about an hour. Make sure you watch the pot and stir it often to prevent it from burning. It will cook down to a nice thin syrup. Let it cool.

In a pitcher, combine the lemon juice and water, then add the watermelon syrup a little at a time, stirring continuously. Serve the lemonade over ice and add a few mint leaves to garnish if you like.

Three Simple Juice Recipes

———————————

I wasn't sure if I should include juice recipes in this book, because I know not everyone has a juicer. But I wanted to cover all bases, just in case you do decide to go all in. If you're debating about what kind of juicer to buy, I recommend investing in a masticating juicer. Masticating juicers generally produce a higher yield and work really well with greens. I also find them easier to clean than centrifugal juicers. Masticating juicers can be a little more costly than some centrifugal models, but in my mind, the higher juice output makes up for the extra expense (as does the easy cleanup). If you decide to buy a masticating juicer, my favorite is the Omega 8006.

I chose a few simple juice recipes to get you started or add to your arsenal. Once you get the hang of it, take it to the next level and experiment with more veggies, like broccoli stalks, fennel, beets, collards, and chard. Get juicing!

Carrot and Orange Juice

MAKES 1 SERVING

1 large orange, peeled

4 carrots, tops removed

1-inch piece of fresh ginger

Juice of 1 small lime

Feed the orange, carrots, and ginger into a juicer. Squeeze lime into the juice and stir. Drink up right away.

KITCHEN NOTES: If you're a ginger lover, you could definitely up the ginger another ½ inch or so for some extra zing.

Green Apple Juice

MAKES 1 SERVING

3 large kale or chard leaves

½ cucumber, cut into spears to fit through the juicer

1 apple, sliced (I like Granny Smith)

2 celery stalks

Handful of cilantro or parsley

Juice of ½ lemon or lime

Feed the greens, cucumber, apple, celery, and cilantro into a juicer. Squeeze lemon or lime into the juice and stir. Drink up right away.

Green Dream Juice

MAKES 1 SERVING

2–3 large handfuls of spinach

1 large cucumber, cut into spears to fit through juicer

1 peeled kiwi, cut into chunks

6–8 strawberries

Big handful of mint or basil (or both)

Juice of 1 small lime

Feed the spinach, cucumber, kiwi, strawberries, and mint and/or basil into a juicer. Squeeze lime into the juice and stir. Drink up right away.

Chocolate Milk/Hot Chocolate

MAKES 2-3 SERVINGS

Pantry Essentials: **NUTS, NATURAL SWEETENER**

This milk is so easy to make and is delicious served hot or cold. Just add all the ingredients to a blender or food processor, and you're done. The peppermint and coconut cream are optional, but they do add a nice holiday vibe during the winter months. I used roasted cashews for this recipe because I think it tastes a little richer with them, but you can easily sub raw cashews if that's what you have on hand.

1 cup unsalted roasted cashews

2½ cups water

4 Medjool dates, pitted and chopped

¼ cup cocoa powder

1 teaspoon peppermint extract (optional)

Coconut cream (page 170; optional)

In a food processor or high-speed blender, grind the cashews until they reach a fine powder. Depending on the speed of your blender or processor, this could take 3 minutes or so. Just make sure you stop before a nut butter starts to form. Add the water, dates, and cocoa powder. If you are adding peppermint extract, do that now too.

You can drink this right away or warm it in a pot over low heat for hot chocolate.

If warming, the milk might thicken a little, so add more water if needed. Pour it into glasses (for cold) or mugs (for hot) and top it with coconut cream if desired.

Resources

Keep going! If you want to learn more about endometriosis, holistic wellness practices, and/or eating and living healthier, I've rounded up some of my favorite books, websites, and films below. Not all of these resources come from a strictly plant-based perspective, but they are all incredible sources of information and inspiration. I'm constantly updating this list, so visit my website, jessicamurnane.com, for the latest.

Endometriosis Resources

Watch:

Endo What? directed by Shannon Cohn, 2016

Read:

The Doctor Will See You Now: Recognizing and Treating Endometriosis by Tamer Seckin, MD

Go Online:

Endometriosis Foundation of America: www.endofound.org

Worldwide Endometriosis March: www.endomarch.org

Food and Wellness Resources

Watch:

Hungry for Change directed by James Colquhoun, Laurentine Ten Bosch, and Carlo Ledesma, 2012

Forks Over Knives directed by Lee Fulkerson, 2013

Cowspiracy: The Sustainability Secret directed by Kip Andersen and Keegan Kuhn, 2014

Food Choices directed by Michal Siewierski, 2016

Fed Up directed by Stephanie Soechtig, 2014

Sugar Coated directed by Michèle Hozer, 2015

Read:

My New Roots by Sarah Britton

The China Study by T. Colin Campbell, PhD, and Thomas M. Campbell II, MD

The Campbell Plan by Thomas M. Campbell II, MD

Crazy Sexy Diet by Kris Carr

Skin Cleanse by Adina Grigore

Fast Food, Good Food by Andrew Weil, MD

Clean Food and *Clean Start* by Terry Walters

YumUniverse by Heather Crosby

Two Moms in the Raw by Shari Koolik Leidich

The Vegetable Butcher by Cara Mangini

Go Online:

mindbodygreen.com

thechalkboardmag.com

wellandgood.com

food52.com

forksoverknives.com

thekitchn.com

Acknowledgments

Cause I got a really big team
And they need some really big rings
They need some really nice things

—DRAKE AND FUTURE

THANK YOU

Amanda Kahle for finding the medicine that changed my life. Endo Resolved for leading the way. Johnny Auer for buying me the first cookbook that really made sense. And Terry Walters for writing that cookbook. Kevin Heineman for a million reasons, but mainly for being you. Al Holleb for crash pads and pep talks. Rachel Holtzman and Marina Birch for always answering my calls.

Sarah Passick for not only being my dream agent, but also my hype-woman, counselor, bodyguard, and friend. Can't imagine doing this (or anything) without you. Jen + Ryan Maconochie for leading me to Sarah. Celeste Fine for making me part of the SLL team.

The Harper Wave crew: Karen Rinaldi for giving this book such a cool home. My incredible editor, Julie Will, for being equal parts nurturing and scary-smart. I brag about you all the time. My (step)editor, Sarah Murphy, for being so kind and open. My copyeditor, Ana Deboo, for making Word track changes cool. Leah Carlson-Stanisic for serifs, stripes, and lots of patience. Joanne O'Neill for a beautiful cover. Brian Perrin for being truly down with OPP. Also, the awesome Victoria Comella, Penny Anna Makras, India Gonzalez, Hannah Robinson, Kate Lyons, and Elizabeth Preske.

Lena Dunham for your open mind, your support, and for being exactly who you are.

Nicole Franzen for being the best photographer, roomie, and friend. Thanks for doing what you do best and also allowing me to do my thing (and not killing me in the process). Vivian Lui and Joni Noe for creating such a beautiful OPP "world"—I want you to style my entire life. John Parot and Anna Billingskog, too! Sarah Britton for nudging me to Nicole and Jane Lee for bringing Joni into my life.

Ramsey Condor for creating such a perfect space and home away from home. Rose Lazar and Bari Ziperstein for your beautiful objects. Ray Blanco for your makeup and brow-taming skills. The Hamiltons and Katie Horwitch for your shoot love.

My fellow-author buds for making this process way more fun and way less *The Shining*. Thanks for all your advice and encouragement. Especially Heather Crosby, Laura Wright, Adina Grigore, Laura Miller, and Andie Mitchell. Also, Erin Gleeson, Phoebe Lapine, Serena Wolf, Megan Silianoff, McKel Hill, Katie Dalebout, and Grace Bonney.

Julia Turshen, Daniel Holzman, Ruth Reichl, Vinson Petrillo, Perry Hendrix, Johnnie Collins, and Owen + Alchemy for contributing recipes. Dr. Thomas Campbell, Maia Hirschbein/California Olive Ranch, Glenn Roberts, Emily Fiffer, Rochelle Bilow, and Whitney Adams for also contributing. Emily Sonnet, Sukey Bernard, and Hickey for the assist.

My recipe testers! This book is better because of you. Special shout to Mac & Murphy, Melissa Sutton, Dana Kauk, and Alissa Ramsay for testing a lot of recipes. Jalen & Jacoby, Malcolm Gladwell, Dan Harris, and Michael Ian Black for keeping me company in the kitchen. Woodland Foods for sending so many great ingredients. The Elliotborough Community Garden for all the free mint. Caviar and Bananas for giving me an "office" where I could write. Sundrops for allowing me to work without worry.

My families: Birch-Pedulla, Thompson, Hayes, Fairdeitch, Jenva, Bozick, Warner, Conrad, Poe, Nichols, Jag, Lyam, Woodward, Scimeca, and Aran. My girls, Coco and Greta. My sisters and brothers (Alissa, Kellie, Abbey, Christopher, Nick, Brandon, and Austin) for being constant inspiration and never knocking anyone's dreams. Mom for coming to help when I needed it most. My in-law-parents, Reen + Tom, because you always say "yes" and with a smile. Deb for winning the Woman of the Year award. You AMAZE me. Dad, for reality checks, other kinds of checks, and teaching me how to write a book way before I even knew I was going to.

To my podcast, website, and newsletter family, you're a big reason I even have the opportunity to write these pages. Your love and support never goes unnoticed. You're truly the best, and I love you so much.

My Sid. How are you so cool? Your spirit changed the way I see the world. Now that *this* book is finished, I promise to finally make your baby book.

My Dan. How are you so great? You make every single day feel like vacation. Thanks for all the big and little things you do for us.

My endo sisters. I see you. I have your back. Let's work together to educate the next generation of women. This disease will not stop us. We won't let it.

One last note. This was the hardest page to write, because I want to acknowledge everyone who's inspired or helped me with OPP. But that's a lot of people and would require an entire second book to list them all. So...I stuck with my family and the people that helped make this book happen. And then made the longest acknowledgment page in history on my website. Please head there for the complete list of people that I want to thank. Like, please, go do it now. I feel a lot of anxiety about not listing everyone here.

Index

NOTE: Page numbers in italics indicate a photograph.

About the Author

Jessica Murnane is a wellness advocate, podcast host, and creator of the One Part Plant movement. She has a certification in plant-based nutrition from the T. Colin Campbell Foundation and works to raise awareness for endometriosis and women's health issues. Jessica has contributed to and appeared in countless magazines and websites, including *Mind Body Green*, *Coveteur*, *Food 52*, *PopSugar*, and *Chalkboard Magazine* and has spoken at Apple and Taste Talks. She interviews some of the biggest names in food, lifestyle, and design on the popular One Part Podcast. Through her website (jessicamurnane.com), events, and restaurant partnerships, she's working to get everyone on this planet to start eating one plant-based meal each day. She lives in Charleston, South Carolina, with her husband, son, and lots of palm trees.